therapy
ACCORDING TO GOD

Rabbi Mordechai Wecker and Michael S. Weissman, PhD

therapy
ACCORDING TO GOD

A Rabbi and a Psychologist
Discuss Life

Mosaica Press, Inc.
© 2019 by Mosaica Press
Typeset by Brocha Mirel Strizower

ISBN-10: 1-946351-58-X
ISBN-13: 978-1-946351-58-6

All rights reserved. No part of this book may be used or reproduced or transmitted in any form or by any means, electronic or mechanical, including photocopying, recording, or by any information storage and retrieval system, without written permission from the publisher.

Published by:
Mosaica Press, Inc.
www.mosaicapress.com
info@mosaicapress.com

In loving memory

JOSEPH ANTIN A"H

17 Tishrei 5716

FLORIA ANTIN A"H

30 Sivan 5715

ALBERT CHAIM ANTIN A"H

14 Tamuz 5711

May they be bound in the bonds of eternal life.

BY THE ANTIN FAMILY TRUST

In memory of my parents

RABBI MEIR MOSHE DAYANIM

and

REBETZIN TAVAS DAYANIM

BY TRUDY AND DR. BEHROOZ DAYANIM

Dedicated in honor of

RABBI MORDECHAI WECKER, SHLITA

with much admiration and gratitude for inspiring and teaching me

Your student and friend

SHOLOM GOODMAN

In loving memory of our dear parents
HERBERT GOODMAN a"h • MARCIA GOODMAN a"h

In loving memory of our dear grandparents
HARRY AND ROSE GOODMAN a"h
JULIUS AND REBECCA FRIEDMAN a"h
IRVING AND ROSE HONIKMAN a"h
TZVI AND ESTHER NEWMAN a"h

SHOLOM AND AVIVA GOODMAN

To
RABBI MORDECHAI WECKER

Bracha v'hatzlacha on this achievement!

ROBERT AND HANNAH KLEIN

THANK YOU FOR BEING MY TEACHER

COUSIN BENJAMIN LIPSCHUTZ

In memory of

MORRIS AND CELIA WEKER
HENRY AND ELIZABETH STERN

Zichronum Liv'racha

DR. WAYNE AND DEBORAH STERN

הרב נפתלי יהודה הלוי הורוויץ
בן הרה"צ לוי יצחק זצוק"ל - דער באסטאנער רבי
Grand Rabbi Naftali Y. Horowitz

ב"ה

יום ג' שנכפל בו כי טוב, טו"ב למטמוני"ם, תשע"ח

לידידי היקר והחשוב, הרב מרדכי ווקר שליט"א

שמחתי לשמוע כי הנך עומד להוציא את הספר 'תורת אמת – חיים אמיתיים', אשר כל כולו נועד לעזור ולהקל על חולי הנפשות המתקשים לנהל חייהם בשלווה ובנחת, ממיטב נסיונו של הר"ר ד"ר מיכאל וויסמן הי"ו העוסק בפסיכולוגיה קלינית כבר ארבעים שנה, והוספת עליו בתוספת מרובה מקורות ממרחבי תורתנו הק', ותורת ה' תמימה משיבת נפש כי היא חכמתנו ובינתנו. וכאשר הנני מכירך בהיותך מלפנים מתפללי בית מדרשנו בית פינחס אזי בטח לבי בכוונתך הטובה לאמיתה של תורה, ותורת חסד על לשונך.

והנני בברכה מרובה כי תזכה לרוב סייעתא דשמיא בכל עניני הוצאת הספר, ויזכה למלא ייעודו ותפקידו לעזור ולהקל לאלו הזקוקים לו, יפוצו מעיינותיך חוצה, ותזכה לרוב ברכה והצלחה בכל מעשי ידיך.

אהל משה
Congregation Ohel Moshe
Rabbi Zvi Teichman, Rabbi
410 570 3333 Email:ravzt@ohelmoshebaltimore.com

July 9, 2018

Dear Reb Mordechai,

I was quite honored by your request of me to pen approbation of your masterful manuscript, Real Torah…Real Life.

Who am I to assess the work of someone whose long history of achievement in the field of Jewish education speaks for itself in the lives of the numerous students you have inspired and enriched through your passionate teaching, artful articulation, vast erudition, and persona that reflects the very 'Real Torah' that is fused into your being, that radiates forth in your every interaction with the world around you.

It is evident from your work, that you are not only a superlative teacher but an avid student of humanity, seeking to fathom the complexities of daily life, enlightening them through the prism of our brilliant Torah.

Your fascinating presentation contrasting the case studies of the esteemed therapist, Dr. Michael S. Weissman, who so skillfully presents the universal array of issues we each face daily, with the Torah's understanding and approach towards curing those ills, as so poignantly transmitted in your skilled hands, has been a most enjoyable and informative read.

I have no doubt this work will prod many to effective and positive change in their lives, continuing your remarkable legacy of elevating all those who enter your sphere.

May you continue to enlighten the world with your brilliant observations and penetrating teachings.

With much admiration, appreciation and friendship,

Zvi Teichman

B'NAI ISRAEL CONGREGATION

420 Spotswood Avenue • Norfolk, VA 23517 • (757) 627-7358 • (757) 627-8544 (fax) • e-mail: office@bnaiisrael.org • www.bnaiisrael.org

Sender Haber
Rabbi

Israel Bornstein ז״ל
Rabbi Emeritus

Jeffrey Brooke
President

Gedalia Schwartz, O.D.
First Vice President

Michael Mostofsky
Second Vice President

Shmuel Itzhak
Treasurer

Ken Wilson
Recording Secretary

Robert Gutterman
Financial Secretary

Michael Weissman, PhD
Past President

Rabbi Mordechai Lolterman
Shmuel Itzhak
Rabbi Sholom Mostofsky
Gabbaim

Bruce Berman
Henry Berman*
Allen S. Bridge, DDS*
Harold Goodman*
Yehudah Leib Griffin
Shmuel Itzhak
J. Leonard Kahn*
Joseph Klein*
Paul Mansheim, MD
William Mazel*
Joseph Miller
Faivich Rabinovich*
Benn Richels
Morton Samuels*
Sidney Siegel*
Barney Siegel
Jordan Slone
Samuel Stamm*
Robert M. Stein
Ludwig Sternlicht, MD
Michael S. Weissman, PhD
Ken Wilson
Melvin Wine*
Avram Zysman
Past Presidents

* *of blessed memory*

August 30, 2018
19 Elul, 5778

ב״ה

Shalom U'vracha,

When two talented men dedicate their lives to helping others, the knowledge and experience that they accumulate is priceless.

I have gained from the wisdom of Rabbi Wecker and Dr. Weissman both personally and in my role as Rabbi at B'nai Israel Congregation in Norfolk, VA.

Rabbi Wecker has studied with and worked closely with some of the greatest Torah minds of our time including Rav Moshe Feinstein, Rav Soloveitchik and Rav Henoch Leibowitz. He has applied his knowledge and clear mindedness to decades of Jewish Education. He inspires and serves as a role model to Jews of all ages.

Dr. Weissman is a therapist's therapist, with prestigious training, unparalleled devotion, and a very deep understanding of the human mind. Rather than try to reconcile psychotherapy with Torah, he has taken the time to study and understand the timeless advice found in the Torah in and use it to make his therapy even more effective.

This book is more than a collaboration. It is a practical demonstration of the wisdom that the Torah has to offer for real world problems. Written with a respect for the Torah and feet firmly planted in the real world and its challenges, this book explores concepts that will be helpful to all serious readers.

May this book be a step forward in repairing all that is broken in this world, and may we live to see a day in which we can confront our challenges effectively as G-d himself wipes away our tears.

Respectfully,

Sender Haber
Rabbi
Bnai Israel Congregation
Norfolk, VA

DAVID H. ROSMARIN, PhD, ABPP
Director, Spirituality & Mental Health Program, McLean Hospital
Assistant Professor, Harvard Medical School

Sunday, July 15th, 2018

I extend a hearty congratulations to Rabbi Mordechai Wecker and Dr. Michael Weissman for their contribution *Therapy According to G-d: A Rabbi and a Psychologist Discuss Life* (Mosaica Press, 2018).

For the majority of the 20th Century, the combined mental health disciplines regarded spirituality as irrelevant. Over the past three decades, the tide has turned as volumes of published scientific research continually demonstrate the key importance of spiritual life to emotional and behavioral wellbeing. As a result, the field has started to embrace spirituality in clinical practice. However, Jewish perspectives and approaches remain at the sidelines.

This wonderful text showcases Torah wisdom as a venerable source to inform clinical intervention. The authors demonstrate how Torah principles can provide real-world solutions to common struggles in the realms of marriage, child rearing, emotional health, and character development. Furthermore, the authors' creative approach of alternating between rabbinic and psychological perspectives throughout the text, highlights the unique and wonderful synergy that is created when clergy and mental health professionals collaborate.

It is my hope that this book will not only be widely read, and not only provide readers with inspiration and practical advice for dealing with common problems, but garner broader interest in Torah as a celebrated and revered repository for psychological wisdom.

With warm regards,

David H. Rosmarin

I am delighted that I was given the opportunity to review Therapy According to G-d, which is validated by many empirically derived findings in cognitive neuroscience and constructs in psychodynamic psychiatry. Importantly, the book affirms a remarkable consistency and complementarity between traditional religious values in general, Torah values in particular, and an eclectic psychotherapeutic approach that promotes adaptive change, enhanced self-esteem and restructuring of character. The Torah provides ample examples in the lives of the patriarchs and matriarchs, judges, kings and prophets of difficult struggles between basic libidinal and aggressive instinctual drives, encompassed by the Yetzer Hara, and the moral conscience, a restraining influence that forces us to pause, reflect, and elect to choose a path that may be difficult, but one that promotes social harmony and inner peace, referred to as the Yetzer Tov. The Talmud and the major expositors of traditional Jewish texts recognized these struggles and wisely concluded that the character of Man is reflected in his/her successful struggle with the Yetzer Hara and, somewhat surprisingly, the greater the character of a Man is the greater is his struggle with his Yetzer Hara, providing the sobering and, potentially, comforting thought that no man or woman is immune from this struggle. Many of the mitzvot have a very real and practical clinical application, they cause us to pause and place conscious reflection between impulse and action, which is often a core therapeutic goal of gaining cognitive control over our intensely felt and experienced emotions. The mitzvot also promote closeness between couples, friends and community by requiring us to think before we speak because thoughtless and frivolous speech can have many unintended hurtful consequences. In any event, this book is an example of a healthy and respectful collaboration between two professionals, one engaged professionally in full-time secular and the other full-time religious pursuits. The collaboration emerged out of Dr. Michael S. Weissman's attendance at an early Saturday morning class on the weekly Torah portion given by Rabbi Mordechai Wecker, which confirmed for both the observations that Torah can have frequent relevance to scholarly secular pursuits and, equally importantly, insights into Torah can often be learned from seemingly exclusively secular activities. Their insights will have practical relevance for many individuals engaged in daily struggle with intra- and interpersonal issues, including those who are already religiously affiliated, those engaged in "searching" or "yearning" for a belief in a Higher Power, and even those who are comfortable with their agnosticism or atheism. The truths and "therapeutic" recommendations have been empirically collected over a three thousand year history, applied effectively, and enjoyed universally. Because the messages contained are timeless and not confined to a particular place, I predict the vignettes, teaching and guidance contained in Therapy According to G-d will be enjoyed broadly by religiously affiliated and unaffiliated readers alike!

Kol HaKovod Dr. Weissman and Rabbi Wecker,

Stephen I. Deutsch, M.D., Ph.D.
Anne Armistead Robinson Endowed Chair in Psychiatry
Professor and Chairman, Department of Psychiatry and Behavioral Sciences

Table of Contents

Acknowledgments XV

Introduction 1

ONE: Our Marriage Is Falling Apart 7
   "Please fix him" 15
   "We don't know who to fix—or whether we want to" 23

TWO: My Kid Is Broken, Please Fix Him 26
   "He thinks just having him live with us will make him behave" 32
   "Do as I say, not as I do" 36
   "We don't see eye to eye on most things, including how to parent" 39

THREE: No One in Our Family Gets Along 44
   "We don't even spend time together like we used to" 49
   "His Mom moved here to help, and now she's the problem" 61
   "She puts everything else before me" 64

FOUR: They Tell Me I Have an Anger Problem 69
   "We can't even talk about this issue without arguing" 75
   "I'll give you what you want, just don't expect me to change" 84

"One step forward, two steps back" 87

Success (or so it seems) 90

"I've finally had it—I'm done dealing with his anger"..............94

*"Wouldn't you be angry if everyone in your life
always messed everything up?"* 100

FIVE: I Don't Know Why I'm So Depressed......................106

"Nothing gives me any pleasure anymore"......................111

*"I'm the one who does everything around here—
if I didn't, nothing would get done"* 117

"No matter how hard I try, I never feel appreciated"..............124

SIX: Middos: Where Torah and Therapy Come Together..........131

Tikkun ha'middos—perfecting ourselves 136

Gaavah (Arrogance) versus Anavah (Humility)............141

Taavah (Lust) versus Gevurah (Strength) 146

Kinah (Jealousy) versus Sippuk (Satisfaction).............149

Kaas (Anger) versus Yishuv Ha'daas (Being Settled)........158

Tikkun ha'olam—perfecting the world 166

Eved Hashem—to be a servant to G-d 174

IN CLOSING: Derech Eretz 179

Acknowledgments

THE AUTHORS DEDICATE THIS BOOK TO those whose continued encouragement and support are responsible for its publication.

To Rabbi Yaacov Haber, Rabbi Doron Kornbluth, and the entire Mosaica Press staff for your guidance, patience, and expertise.

To those who wrote *haskamahs* and letters of recommendation for the book. Thank you so much!

To you, dear reader. We hope these lessons will resonate with you. May Hashem bless you and support you in your quest for *gadlus* (spiritual greatness).

To Hakadosh Baruch Hu, for the innumerable blessings He has bestowed upon us and our families, and for His Torah—the source of all wisdom.

Rabbi Wecker acknowledges the following people:

To my wife, Chana, who models the *middos tovos* discussed in this book. You serve as my constant inspiration to serve Hashem, may He be blessed, and to act with *menschlichkeit*.

To all my children and their spouses, my grandchildren, and my mother-in-law, for your encouragement and patience as I wrote and rewrote the text. Each of you, in his/her own way, models joy and commitment to our sacred *mesorah*.

To those whose financial sponsorship made this publication possible. I greatly value your friendship and support.

Dr. Weissman acknowledges the following people:

To Brina, my "bride of forty-seven years," who, through her wisdom and love, has been an endless source of support, guidance, and when needed, *mussar*. She is the miracle of my life.

To my son, Eric, who has been an endless source of *nachas*, and his wife, Julie, whose dedication of purpose and amazing competence as a mother to two unbelievable children is an inspiration. And to my precious daughter, Sara, exuding love and caring since she was born and who opened the gates for her mother and me to begin our path back to Torah Judaism. And to her husband, Rabbi Gershon Litt, whose dedication to *kiruv* and extraordinary gift of touching others in a way which awakens their *pintele Yid* has led scores of Jews to a life of Torah. And to their five scholarly and loving sons who collectively are role models to their peers and loved by their teachers.

To the *rebbeim* who have most guided me: Rabbi Joseph Ehrenkranz, *zt"l*, Rabbi Yosef Friedman, Rabbi Aaron Baer, *zt"l*, and Rabbi Sender Haber.

Introduction

THE TORAH. THE "BLUEPRINT FOR THE UNIVERSE." The "owner's manual," giving us instructions as to how we should live our lives. The oldest document in continuous use in all recorded history. G-d's gift to the Jews, His chosen people.

However, it's not simply a gift. It's a gift with a "catch" attached. Not actually a catch but more accurately a task attached to the gift: we must live our lives according to the laws and rules contained in it. By doing so, we become "a light unto the nations," a beacon focused on bringing all of humanity to a closer relationship with G-d. Our mission is not only to learn His Torah, and in so doing, strive to be closer to Hashem, but we must also implement Torah truths as we interact with the world. As G-d's chosen people, we have a responsibility to dedicate ourselves to *tikkun ha'middos*—to perfect ourselves, and to *tikkun olam*—to repair and improve the world.

Still, the Torah is much more than that. It is G-d making Himself known to the world: the Revelation. That moment in time is the essence of the Jewish People, indeed, of every Jew. It has been our lifeblood for over three thousand years. It's what sustains us, keeps us alive, and gives us our sense of purpose in the world. It is eternal.

It is also high drama. We see in the lives of our forebears how relationships and stories unfold; these capture our basic nature, an animalistic body with needs and drives and the entire range of human emotions, bound up with a spiritual core, a holy and pure *neshamah*, our soul. There appears to be an eternal conflict between these two warring parts—the *yetzer ha'tov* (the "good inclination"), constantly fending off the seductive techniques, and the *yetzer ha'ra* (the "evil inclination"), challenging our will to follow what G-d expects us to do.

This war between our physical nature and our soul is a war played out within each of us. It is also a constant undercurrent in the larger arena of human relationships. The Torah tells us of these relationships, both to help us understand our roots, our heritage, and our culture, and as a vehicle to convey eternal truths about how we must live and grow and evolve, constantly improving ourselves, refining our character traits, and most importantly, conducting ourselves in a way which helps us achieve the ultimate goal of growing closer to G-d.

In this book, we attempt to bring the eternal principles of living as espoused in the Torah to the practical level, by illustrating how these principles can be incorporated into our daily lives. We will also see the illustrations of the consequences when one chooses a lifestyle which ignores some of these timeless principles. We see these sad and often disastrous consequences in many places. Jewish history is replete with examples of what can—and does—happen when these principles are abandoned. We see it in our modern culture, with an unprecedented breakdown in morality. We see it in the progressive breakdown of the traditional family and in the violence that erupts all around us. We see it in the high divorce rate and in unbridled consumerism which makes *what you have* more important than *who you are*. We see it in the increasingly widespread symptoms of human malaise—depression, drug and alcohol abuse, anxiety, troubling dropout rates from school, and even in the deterioration of values and ethical conduct in our leaders.

We have chosen a particular setting to explore in detail how important these principles are in each individual's adaptation to daily living. It is a setting in which individuals and families come to get help dealing with life problems. They come to deal with such distressing symptoms as anxiety, depression, anger issues, family conflict, and substance abuse. They come blaming others—their parents, their spouse, their children, their job, their finances, events from the past, and so on. What they usually do not know, but will come to know, is that they are really coming to work on developing *their* character traits, to learn to take responsibility for *their* actions and decisions and how *they* impact everyone they come into contact with. What they don't know is that it is *their own character traits* which are at the core of the "presenting problem" and *their own ways of coping* with life situations. We will come to see that these character traits and faulty coping mechanisms actually create most, if not all, of the problem, and that the "corrective maneuvers" which are necessary to address the problem involve insights about themselves which invariably are rooted in fundamental Torah principles and how to properly apply them. The setting we have chosen to achieve this level of insight is the psychotherapist's office.

It is important to note that because these Torah principles about how to conduct one's life are universal, the person seeking the therapist's help may never know—at least explicitly—that the new tools they are learning to cope with life are rooted in the eternal Torah. Indeed, the psychotherapy process as practiced by Dr. Weissman utilizes all the diagnostic and treatment approaches used by licensed mental health professionals. Most patients seeking help are not Jewish, but they know that Dr. Weissman is Jewish, primarily because of his yarmulke. A surprising number of non-Jewish patients express interest in the "Jewish roots" of some of our work, such that we can even have an explicit discussion that might include direct reference to halachah (Jewish law) or Jewish philosophy, or even on occasion examples from Jewish biblical sources. More often no direct reference is made to the fact that the therapeutic interventions are derived from his understanding of Jewish law, which, for the most part, is consistent with and at the root of most of the major principles in psychology.

In Western society, there is a tendency to view one's religious life as separate and distinct from how one lives his daily life. It is sort of a personalized version of "separation of church and state." This book was written as a vehicle to help bridge the gap between what many consider part of their religious life and the actual ways in which we *choose* to live. Human beings are the only creatures on Earth with the power of choice, of free will. Yes, the key word here is "choose." Individuals who seek the help of the psychotherapist can learn that an active process of embracing—and living—these principles is both the cure for their malaise and the foundation which can lead to a fulfilling life with a sense of purpose and inner peace. Even if an individual expresses no interest in any form of religion in their life, the eternal truths we find in the Torah are no less applicable as tools to guide one's choices and actions.

The genesis of this book stems from a friendship which developed between Rabbi Wecker, a Torah scholar whose life has been dedicated to learning and teaching Torah in a wide range of Jewish institutes of learning, and Dr. Weissman, a psychotherapist who has been in practice for forty years, who embraced a Torah way of life twenty years ago and who has come to see that everything of value in the transformative work in psychotherapy is directly linked to the principles and statutes of the Torah. This friendship developed during the three years Rabbi Wecker lived in Norfolk, Virginia, serving as Head of School of the Hebrew Academy of Tidewater. During those years Rabbi Wecker offered a Shabbos morning class on the weekly *parashah*, which the attendees found to be inspiring, profound, and filled with Rabbi Wecker's unique sense of humor. As one of those regular attendees, Dr. Weissman found innumerable connections between the Torah as conveyed and interpreted by Rabbi Wecker and what takes place in the psychotherapist's office. Rabbi Wecker's classes were inspired by his own observations and interpretations from each *parashah*, which were always supported by his well-researched sources, and by his gifted recall of years of learning as a *talmid* of Rav Moshe Feinstein, zt"l, Rav Henoch Leibowitz, zt"l, and other esteemed rabbinic authorities.

Both during classes and in other settings (often around the Shabbos table), our conversations seemed to continuously augment each other's knowledge and experience base, with the result that it was natural to see if we could capture the insights which emerged into a form which could be shared with others. The title of this work, *Therapy According to G-d*, conveys the underlying theme of this work, namely, to show how G-d's Torah emerges constantly in the clinical setting of the psychotherapist's office, which itself is a microcosm of life's struggles shared to some degree by all of us, offering the very basis of any and every therapeutic intervention.

The format of this book reflects the primary goal we hope to achieve, which is to share insights gleaned from the psychotherapy office and to present those insights in a way that conveys the inseparable connection between "G-d's instruction manual" for how to live and the therapeutic interventions which result in real life changes. We have chosen to organize this volume according to "categories" of issues which present in the therapy office, which correspond to life situations faced by all of us. Of course, the categories overlap in many ways. An individual with an alcohol problem impacts many others, both within his family and beyond. A depressed or anxious mother impacts her entire family. At the same time, a dysfunctional family can generate a wide range of maladaptive behavioral patterns in each of the family members. The interface between the school or job and home can be fraught with complications. One person's physical—or mental—illness can have dramatic effects on the family. Conversely, any of the above problem situations can be seen as an opportunity for growth and improvement, but only if the right "ingredients" are put in. And, of course, those "ingredients" are found in the Torah. Therefore, our format will revolve around several different "categories" of issues, and throughout the narrative of the clinical material from Dr. Weissman's therapy office, Rabbi Wecker will offer Torah insights that convey how Torah pervades all aspects of personal growth, offering tools to address and resolve life's challenges, and the path to the achievement of a fulfilling life.

In keeping with the central premise of this book, namely how Torah principles can be applied in the real-life situations which persons in distress bring to the psychotherapist's office, Rabbi Wecker will intersperse the real-life clinical situations presented by Dr. Weissman with a discussion of Torah thoughts which relate to the clinical vignettes. We will also come to see how the psychotherapist's office can, and often should, work closely with the spiritual guidance that can be found in the rabbi's office.

The reader should note that all clinical material presented in this volume carefully disguises the identity of any individual, family, workplace, school, etc., but all the clinical vignettes are based on actual interactions in the psychotherapy office.

CHAPTER ONE

Our Marriage Is Falling Apart

"I KNOW WE LOVE EACH OTHER, *but we don't know how to talk to each other. Every time we try, it turns into an argument and we get nowhere.*"

"*He just doesn't understand me. He doesn't care about my feelings, and when I try to tell him what I'm feeling, it doesn't seem to matter to him.*"

"*As soon as I walk through the door, she hits me with all the stuff that's been bothering her all day. Doesn't she understand that when I come home from work I just need to chill? Besides, it's always the same stuff she wants to talk about—how she feels about this and how she feels about that. It's always the same.*"

These are some of the issues couples bring to therapy. Inevitably, when I dig a little bit deeper by asking them to explain exactly what happens during their attempt to communicate, the focus changes from "we" to "I":

> "I don't know if he loves me the way he used to."
>
> "Whenever I want some affection, she's not interested."
>
> "I work hard to earn money. All she wants to do is spend it."

Upon closer examination, the "I statements" reveal embedded "You statements." There is always some direct or implied accusation about the other person's competence, judgment, indifference, lack of desire for affection, or more. I almost never hear (at least not in the first session!) something like "It pains me to see her sad," or "I'm worried because he's so tired when he gets home that he doesn't seem to enjoy anything anymore."

As we saw above, this couple began their very first session by saying, "We know we love each other, but…" Whenever a husband and wife proclaim their love for each other and then immediately go on to say how they cannot talk and it's the other person's fault, one must wonder about each person's understanding of "love." Quite often, at the earliest stage of therapy, it is helpful to begin the process of helping these couples in distress by questioning how each of them understands the concept of "love."

Rabbi Wecker

There are differing views on exactly how old Avraham Avinu was when he "discovered G-d," i.e., when he became convinced of the existence of the One Creator and Sustainer of the universe. The Talmud claims he was three years old.[1] The *Zohar* states:

> In the morning he saw the sun rise in the east and felt certain that the sun was the king who created him. When the evening came and the moon shined, he transferred his allegiance to the moon. When the sun returned the next morning, he realized that there was in reality a Supreme Being Who directed the sun, the moon, and the rest of creation according to His will.[2]

---

1 *Nedarim* 32a.
2 *Zohar* 1:86a.

Another source notes that Avraham was either forty-eight or fifty years old when he discovered G-d.[3] Avraham is referred to as Avraham HaIvri, Avraham the Hebrew, for the rest of the world was on one side of the river while Avraham stood on the opposite side (*eiver*, the "other side" [of the river], comes from the same root as *ivri*).[4] Avraham is portrayed here as someone who single-handedly challenged the conventional wisdom and religious tenets of his time. He was virtually alone in his belief in monotheism.

What was G-d's response to Avraham's quest? Silence. G-d did not appear to Avraham in a prophetic vision or confirm his beliefs in any other way. The very first communication G-d had with Avraham is recorded at the beginning of *Parashas Lech Lecha*, when Avraham was seventy-five years old, many years after his discovery of G-d's existence. Even then, G-d did not provide him with any type of confirmation or even an introduction. All He said was *"Lech lecha"*—Leave your homeland!

This scenario contrasts with the introduction G-d made to Moshe when He communicated with him for the first time at the burning bush. There G-d introduced Himself as the G-d of Avraham, Yitzchak, and Yaakov.

Why did G-d not reveal Himself earlier to Avraham, and confirm to him that he was indeed on the right track?

Rav Yosef Dov Soloveitchik[5] answered that each person is endowed with a *yetzer ha'tov*, a "good inclination," often understood to be synonymous with a conscience. We do not require a prophecy to convince us of the correctness of our moral choices. We possess an inner voice that can fine-tune our direction in life if we are responsive to it. Avraham's inner sensitivity served to confirm his choices to him—he did not need outside validation.

So why did Moshe receive an introduction? Perhaps the reason that G-d provided Moshe with an introduction was to strengthen his resolve to carry out his mission to free the Jewish People from enslavement in Egypt and lead them for the rest of his life.

---

3   *Pesikta Rabbasi* 21:18.
4   *Bereishis Rabbah* 42:13.
5   Rosh Yeshiva at Yeshiva University in New York City. He lived from 1903 to 1993.

The *Gra*[6] notes that during the time of the *nevi'im* (prophets), a person needing spiritual direction could meet with a *navi* (prophet) who would pinpoint the exact area of serving Hashem that he needed to stress and the direction in life that he should follow.[7] With the cessation of prophecy, *ruach ha'kodesh* (Divine inspiration) was passed on to every one of us. We can, if we are totally honest with ourselves, be inspired to do the right thing and follow the specific path that G-d has designated for us.

In light of the myriad pitfalls of this approach, though, it is essential to find an appropriate mentor who can help guide us with the light of Torah, halachah, and Jewish tradition. Hashem has provided us with the guides and guideposts, and the inspiration and motivation to do what is right, thereby enabling us to become fulfilled as faithful Jews. The choice is ours to make, and with His support, we will lead meaningful, productive, and happy lives.

There is something mysterious in the Torah way of life that makes sense to us, that addresses us on a deeply profound level. Rav Henoch Leibowitz[8] referred to the Torah as the "elixir of life." All we need to do is appreciate what we have and we will be truly content.

SUMMARY

Each person is endowed with a yetzer ha'tov, a "good inclination" or a conscience. We do not require a prophecy to convince us of the correctness of our moral choices. We possess an inner voice that can fine-tune our direction in life if we are responsive to it. Our failure to make appropriate choices has a negative impact on our neshamos (souls), and we are (on some level) self-aware of our failures and their repercussions.

Dr. Weissman

The first clinical vignette illustrates how easy it is to fall into a pattern of behavior in a marriage in which both the husband and

---

6   The acronym of the *Vilna Gaon*, HaGaon Rabbeinu Eliyahu Kramer of Vilna, Lithuania, considered by many to be the foremost Torah scholar of his time. He lived from 1720 to 1797.
7   Commentary on *Mishlei* 16:4.
8   Rosh Yeshiva of Yeshiva Chofetz Chaim, in Queens, New York. He lived from 1918 to 2008.

wife, in different ways, don't "listen" to their *yetzer ha'tov* but only see things through the filter of wanting their own needs met. They each really "know" that their own behaviors are hurtful to the other, yet they blame each other even as they proclaim their love.

> *We're coming to therapy because we both don't want a divorce. We really love each other, but we have huge communication problems. We don't know how to talk to each other without fighting, and ultimately, screaming at each other. One time it even looked like my husband was coming close to hitting me, but he immediately stopped himself and I knew right away that he felt badly about that. I know he'll never hurt me, at least not physically, but we can't seem to be together without fighting.*

Mrs. Kline went on to say that her husband constantly questions her about whether she has gotten things done around the house, which she feels is an attack. She said that she takes care of all the housework and childcare, yet he always sees her as inadequate—"without showing any appreciation for how difficult it is for me to get everything done, given my struggle with ADHD"—and that she despairs of ever meeting his standards. She knows that whenever he questions her in this manner, she becomes very hurt and defensive. She feels that he is too demanding and controlling, with excessively high expectations of her and others, and she resents that if the house is not exactly the way he wants it to be, she "gets in trouble." She is also anxious about his potential to explode in an angry outburst.

At this point, Mr. Kline began to explain his point of view.

> *I would like it if when I come home from work, she would at least have the house somewhat in order, with dinner prepared, and her having already bathed the kids and taken her own shower. I want her to be dressed and "look nice" for me—so we can enjoy quiet time together after the kids are in bed.*

He has an image of how things should be at home. He feels that she really could do a better job and that his expectations are reasonable. He would like her to cook, clean, be a stay-at-home mom, have dinner ready, and have the children taken care of and "not too disruptive" when they sit down to dinner. They have two children—a three-year-old daughter and a one-year-old son.

As I listened to these two intelligent adults describe the misery in their marriage, I found myself stuck on how both of them emphasized how much they "love" each other. In Hebrew, the word for "love" is *ahavah*, which literally means "to give." I inquired as to what each of them believes to be the definition of "love," and after some discussion, one of them stated that it means to care about the other person. The other took longer to respond and eventually struggled to explain that love has to do with feeling that you're special and important to the other person. I suggested another way to look at it—that "love" is best understood as a verb, not a noun, and that love is something that you **do**, not what you **feel** (or think you feel). It means to give to the other. When asked for examples of how they actively demonstrate their love for the other, both husband and wife readily admitted that they have been very remiss in terms of thinking about how much they are **giving** to the other and instead have been focusing on how much they feel they are not **getting** from the other.

When confronted with the question of how they feel about themselves when they say something hurtful to each other, Mr. Kline (who previously admitted that he has anger management issues) blurted out that he feels terrible. We discussed how demeaning his wife—always making her feel insufficient and focusing only on his needs and not on hers—is in fact demeaning himself. Despite his anger issues, he has always thought of himself as a loving person, the kind of person whose self-concept is rooted in being the guy who will help a friend out in a pinch and will work hard to provide for his family. Yet, feeling entitled to verbally demean the person he says he loves the most is a way of renouncing some of the most important aspects of what makes him human, created in G-d's image. He becomes a slave to his needs and feelings of the moment, not pausing to reflect on the impact of his words, or even the fact that he has a **choice** as to how to respond to frustrations. He needs to learn how to treat his wife in a way that elevates him, that reflects his own deeply held values—values he has been neglecting in his interactions with his wife, but nonetheless values which, not surprisingly, reflect some eternal principles that emanate from the Torah.

We all have intuitive knowledge as to whether our actions are truly in keeping with our imbedded inclination to do "good," and this knowledge should guide us as we make decisions about how to treat others. Rabbi Wecker takes this further with the next *d'var Torah*, which stresses the importance of treating everyone—including ourselves—with the kind of respect that is in keeping with the recognition that we are all created in the image of Hashem.

Rabbi Wecker

Bereishis 5:1 states: "This is the account of the descendants of Adam, on the day of G-d's creation of man; He made him in the likeness of G-d." Rabbi Akiva quotes the verse, "And you shall love your neighbor as yourself,"[9] and comments: This is a significant principle in our Torah. However, the Midrash says that Ben Azzai, another great Torah authority, quotes our verse from *Bereishis* and maintains that it is evocative of an even greater principle.

Da'as Zekanim explains: From the verse quoted by Rabbi Akiva, one may only infer that that which is hateful to me I may not do to my fellow. Ben Azzai adds to that principle fundamentally: He suggests that even if someone is humble or uncaring of his own honor, he must still treat his fellow humans with all due respect and dignity. He must recognize the likeness of G-d in his fellow human even while he chooses not to recognize it in himself. Indeed, Rav Henoch Leibowitz notes that it is only a sense of self-dignity that keeps us from sin. As the sainted Chofetz Chaim comments, "By shaming his fellow, he is but shaming the likeness of G-d Himself."

Ramban claims[10] that the Torah exaggerates a bit when commanding us "to love your neighbor as yourself." Such an ideal, taken literally,

---

9   *Vayikra* 19:18.
10   Ibid.

is not something a person can accept. Indeed, the Talmud rules that one does not have to share his rations with another Jew in a desert if there is only enough sustenance for one person to reach civilization.[11] That ruling, *Ramban* maintains, proves that one need not love another person literally as he loves himself. Instead, the Torah's intent is that we should strive to support another Jew in any way, just as we would do so for ourselves.

Rambam, on the other hand, implies[12] that the Torah is to be taken literally and that one must "love a fellow Jew as himself." Rav Yosef Dov Soloveitchik, following his Brisker family tradition, adopted this interpretation.

It should be noted that even the approach advocated by *Ramban* is challenging to live by. Hashem expects us, according to this view, to honestly and energetically strive to support and advocate for our fellow Jew to the same degree we would for ourselves.

Perhaps this understanding of the mitzvah (commandment) can provide a deeper understanding of a famous incident involving the great rabbi Hillel. The Talmud relates[13] that after being rebuffed by Shammai, a non-Jew approached Hillel and asked to be taught the entire Torah while he stood on one foot. Hillel responded, "What you find hateful, do not do to your fellow. That is the entire Torah and the rest is essential commentary. Go and study it." It seems that Hillel simply reformulated the *pasuk* "Love your neighbor as yourself" in the negative. Why did Hillel formulate the idea in his own words rather than quote the *pasuk*?

Iyun Yaakov explains that the ideal expressed in the *pasuk* may well have been overwhelming for someone contemplating conversion to Judaism. Hillel sought to make the goal seem attainable by putting it in the negative. To avoid doing something that one finds hateful is considerably easier than to actively support another person in any and every way. With continued Torah study, the convert would come to realize the all-encompassing scope of this great mitzvah.

---

11   *Bava Metzia* 62a.
12   *Hilchos Dei'os* 6:3.
13   *Shabbos* 31a.

SUMMARY

We and all of humanity were created in the image of G-d. We are therefore obligated to manifest both self-respect and respect for others. G-d in effect is instructing us that our reputations (and certainly the reputations of others!) are not ours to discard. Our status and character derive from our likeness to Him, may He be blessed, and may not be trifled with.

Dr. Weissman

The following case is replete with examples of how a Torah perspective can resolve and overcome what may appear to be insurmountable obstacles. In keeping with the major thrust of the previous *d'var Torah*, I will place special emphasis on the importance of dealing with challenges to a relationship in a manner that reflects both self-respect and respect for others.

"PLEASE FIX HIM"

> *I really thought my marriage was pretty good, although I guess looking back, my feelings had already begun to fade little by little. My husband is truly a good man. He would give the world for me, although he is kind of cheap when it comes to spending money on vacations and travel. Everyone loves him, both at the church where he serves as a lay minister and at work where everyone respects him. However, I always found him to be clingy and smothering, always hovering around, always wanting a kiss or a hug or some kind of attention. I guess I was already feeling "distant" from him when I discovered how much I enjoyed communicating with my friends over the internet. It started with text messages. I learned how to send a text to several people at once, and that really was exciting for me. In just a "click," we could share everything from recipes to arranging playdates for the kids. Pretty soon we all got onto Facebook, and then WhatsApp, which allowed me to communicate with many more people in the neighborhood, as well as in my church community. I found that the internet, and especially my iPad,*

gave me a sense of being connected, and it opened so many doors I didn't even know existed. I admit, I even started playing interactive games over the internet on my iPad, sometimes with complete strangers who I knew I'd never actually meet. It's gotten to the point where I spend a lot of time chatting with my friends, keeping in touch with many old friends I have not seen in years, and sometimes just searching the internet for interesting articles or information about this or that.

They say it can become kind of addictive, so maybe that's happening to me a little bit. He complains about it all the time, that I don't give enough attention to him or the kids. He's wrong about the kids—I still shop and make meals for everyone, but they're older now and don't need to spend so much time with me. They'd rather be up in their rooms anyway, doing their own thing. And as far as my husband, he just continues to complain and then smother me with his need to always spend time with me. I don't know, I just don't have the same feelings for him. So here I am, hoping you can help me—since I don't know if my husband can change or be different—so I can feel good about being married to him again and interested in spending time with him. I feel stuck! I need to find the motivation to focus on my marriage.

I saw this distressed woman for several weeks, with her continuing to go back and forth in her mind and heart as to what she wanted to do with her marriage. We brought her husband into some of the sessions at those times when she "really wanted to work on her marriage." Meanwhile, she continued with her expanding social activities and her preoccupation with her smartphone and the internet. Her husband was surprisingly tolerant of the situation, even as he complained about it, and he continued to try to show her as much affection and attention as he could, despite her rebuffs. The fact that he was so accepting of the situation seemed to confirm my patient's impression of him as a dependent person without much "backbone." In our sessions, she would waver back and forth—at one moment recognizing the sanctity of marriage and her obligation to fulfill her commitment to be a loving wife, and at the next saying that everyone deserves happiness, and if she would discontinue her internet activities in order to give more attention to the marriage, she would be faking it in ways that would make both of them miserable. Her cognitive dissonance was so strong that even as she was expressing very positive feelings about my work with her, on several occasions she sent me an email canceling future sessions, saying she wanted to work things out on her own. I became the symbol of her cognitive dissonance, in that with me she could not "hide" this ongoing internal conflict. Interestingly, she would always respond positively when I returned her messages with a reminder that "perhaps" she is running from facing her dilemma, and a suggestion that she "change her mind" and continue therapy. Her positive reaction implied that she knew she couldn't escape her internal knowledge that her behaviors were at variance with her deeply held values.

In this woman's highly distressing situation, which brought her to therapy, was an unspoken wish for me to somehow help her find a way to love her husband, since over the years his passivity and tendency to smother her with affection diminished her feelings for him. She had gradually lost her respect for him. Although she wasn't saying this directly, what she wanted was for me to "fix him," to make him into the kind of person she believed she needed in order to be happy in her marriage.

As we follow this patient during the course of her therapy, we will see how actively she tries to resolve her cognitive dissonance. We will come to see how a major "missing ingredient" in this marriage is her recognition that "love" is a verb, something you **do**, not just something you feel. As stated previously, in Hebrew, the word "love," *ahavah*, means "to give." First, let us take another glimpse into the wisdom of the Torah.

Rabbi Wecker

In *Bereishis* 7:13 it says, "On that very day, Noach, Sham, Cham, Yafes, and their wives came into the ark." *Rashi* comments that the *pasuk* teaches you that the people of Noach's generation said, "If we would see Noach entering the ark, we would break it apart and kill him." G-d said, "I will bring him into the ark in full view of them, and we will see whose words will be fulfilled."

In *Bereishis* 17:26 the Torah states, "On that very day Avraham was circumcised, and his son Yishmael was circumcised as well." *Rashi* observes that the *bris milah* took place by day and not by night, and that Avraham was not afraid of the heathens and scoffers. Another reason Avraham was circumcised by day was so that his enemies and contemporaries could not claim: Had we seen him, we would not have permitted him to perform the circumcision to fulfill G-d's command.

Rav Elya Meir Bloch[14] asked: Why were the people of the generations of Noach and Avraham so concerned with the actions of these *tzaddikim*? If they believed in G-d, they should have actively supported the causes espoused by Noach and Avraham. On the other hand, if they were heretics, they should have been apathetic to anything that was said or done by these *tzaddikim*! They should have scoffed at Noach's 120-year construction project and been bemused with the prospect of Noach and his family sitting like fools (in the eyes of the scoffers) in the ark awaiting the start of a flood that the scoffers felt certain would not occur. Similarly, with regard to Avraham, the heretics should have simply mocked the actions of a "crazy old man" subjecting himself to such a painful operation for what in their mind was some silly reason.

The Rosh Yeshiva explained that these people were conflicted: On one hand, they refused to acknowledge the truth of the Torah and its attendant moral code and restrictions. On the other hand, their conscience allowed them no rest over the possibility of the veracity of the Torah.

Therefore, they struck out at the source of their tension: these *tzaddikim*. To allow the plans of these *tzaddikim* to unfold unchallenged would have been too painful for them to contemplate.

There is a popular expression about an atheist who says, "There is no G-d [*chas v'shalom*] and I hate Him! Belief in G-d is the foundation of all morality and the cornerstone of humanity's charge to raise itself spiritually. Denial of G-d is an emotional response from someone who

---

[14] Rosh Yeshiva of Telshe Yeshiva. He lived from 1894 to 1954.

for whatever reason(s) does not want to commit himself to serve Him. Such a person is never at peace with himself and must continually find ways to justify his denial of Hashem.

SUMMARY

Our Torah teaches us that we all innately recognize that we have an obligation to follow the dictates of our Creator. If one chooses to follow in His ways, well and good. If one chooses to rebel against Him (chas v'shalom), he will suffer pangs of conscience that will either cause him to repent or will result in his further alienation from Him in a futile effort to quiet the yetzer ha'tov.

> *I'm finding myself more and more frustrated by so many things lately. Things between my husband and me remain tense and strained. They've cut my hours at church, where I have worked for years as the office manager, from forty hours per week to twenty-eight hours. And the way they treat my husband is unfair; I think the new pastor really takes advantage of him. I've actually stopped going to church recently because of all of this. He continues to go, but I find myself just getting upset there as I think about all the hypocrisy I see. I know I should go, and that I shouldn't confuse the individual person with the whole religion, but I'm finding it all just too difficult to handle right now. I figure I need a break from it all.*

Much like the scorners and heretics in Noach's time, my patient became more actively negative in her attitude toward life—distancing herself from her religious life, more critical of her husband, and ultimately more critical of herself, to the point where she stated that she has "no self-esteem left." She had recently admitted that she still spends a lot of time chatting with her friends and on the internet, and she has come to see this as her escape from her unhappiness at home. She also started to say how she hated to have to come in to therapy each week and "confess." For her, I have become analogous to the requirement that Noach board his ark in daylight and the requirement that Avraham perform his *bris milah* in daylight. When she comes to therapy, we shed light on her internal conflict, and at times that only intensifies her pain. Yet, she remains committed to the process of therapy and to the good therapeutic relationship we have formed, and therefore is to be admired for her willingness to continue to place herself under the spotlight every time she comes to therapy.

We can reframe the core issues in this case from a Torah perspective. The patient is engaged in a "war" between her *yetzer ha'tov*—her deep recognition that it is **she** who is not giving to her husband or the marriage, and her *yetzer ha'ra*—the justification of her pursuit of immediate pleasure and escape. Even more significant is that she "knows" that her *yetzer ha'tov* is giving her the "correct answer," the truth as to where her energy and attention should go. Like Avraham, she knows without question what the right path is. And she knows that choosing the right path is her only way of achieving contentment.

Rabbi Wecker

The Talmud notes that Rabbi Yochanan said, "Greater praise is given to Iyov than that given to Avraham."[15] Concerning Avraham, it is written (after he successfully withstood the test of *Akeidas Yitzchak*), "For now I know that you fear G-d," whereas regarding Iyov, it is written, "He was perfect and upright, and one who feared G-d and turned away from evil." The praise offered to Iyov is more lavish than that offered to Avraham. Why?

Maharsha observes that there is no real implication that Iyov was in fact greater than Avraham. G-d was speaking to Avraham directly when He called him G-d-fearing, while the assessment of Iyov was not made to him personally. We are taught that only a partial praise of a person is made in his presence,[16] presumably in order to avoid contributing to any feelings of conceit by the subject. Thus, Avraham's praises as

---

15   *Bava Basra* 15b.
16   *Eruvin* 18b.

recorded were only a part of the accolades appropriate for him, and he was in fact greater than Iyov.

Maharal comments that more qualities are listed for Iyov than for Avraham because Iyov was a composite of the qualities of Avraham, Yitzchak, Yaakov, and David HaMelech. Apparently, Iyov was the spiritual patriarch of the non-Jewish world.

Radak explains that Avraham's "fear" as expressed in this trial was an expression of love,[17] for he did not fear G-d in the physical sense that one seeks to avoid pain or punishment. Rather, he feared that his soul might be considered unworthy. He loved his son Yitzchak more than himself but was prepared to sacrifice Yitzchak in order to ensure his own continued close relationship with G-d in *Olam Haba* (the Hereafter). Such was Avraham's love of Hashem and his reluctance to forfeit the opportunity to serve Him. Avraham's relationship with Hashem is thus placed on a level far above that of Iyov.

Netziv explains that while Avraham prayed for the people of Sodom at length, he did not plead for the life of his beloved son Yitzchak. Avraham conducted himself as if the *Akeidas Yitzchak* was decreed not by the merciful G-d he knew but by an unkind human king to whom one could not appeal for mercy. Avraham realized that any plea he might make for Yitzchak's life would be interpreted as a deficiency in his relationship with Hashem, and thus create a *chillul Hashem*.

Perhaps the following distinctions can be drawn between the spiritual accomplishments of Avraham and those of Iyov:

- First, Avraham's love of Hashem was of a much greater quality than Iyov's. Love of Hashem is described as the highest level of Divine service, and thus Avraham's stature was clearly greater than that of Iyov. The Talmud's comment is not meant to equate the accomplishments of Avraham and Iyov, but only to suggest some type of connection between their respective attainments of fear of Hashem. Although the accolades offered to Iyov surpassed those offered to Avraham, the assessment of Avraham

---

17   *Bereishis* 22:12.

was made to him personally. Only a partial praise of a person is made in his presence.[18] Thus, Avraham's praises as recorded were only a part of the many accolades due him.

- Second, Avraham was a trailblazer who was propagating and bequeathing to humanity an approach in serving Hashem. All the subsequent accomplishments of individuals in later generations, including those of Iyov, therefore rebounded to his merit.

SUMMARY

The highest level of serving Hashem is love of G-d. One who is on that exalted level is able to subjugate his passions because of their intense affection for G-d. Avraham reached this exalted level of Divine service (and perhaps Iyov did as well, according to some views). Rav Yisrael Salanter[19] pointed out that in his eighteenth-century milieu, it was virtually impossible to find someone on this lofty level. Rav Henoch Leibowitz pointed out that although today we cannot reach this level in totality, we can occasionally experience it in moments of great joy.

Dr. Weissman

The contrast described between Avraham and Iyov can be seen as a paradigm that can be applied to relationships. We just saw that reference to Avraham's "fear" of Hashem is best understood as rooted in a love of Hashem and a desire to serve Him. This quality of Avraham's love for Hashem—the desire to serve Him—can be related to the quality of one's love for his or her spouse.

There is a huge distinction between a possessive or selfish "love" for another person and a more mature form of love, which usually includes the wish to love and give to another person.

There is an interesting anecdote told of a Rosh Yeshiva who passed through the lunchroom of his yeshiva and observed a young *bachur* (student) eating his lunch with great zeal and obvious enjoyment. The Rosh

---

18   *Eruvin* 18b.
19   Known as the father of the Mussar Movement. He lived from 1810 to 1883.

Yeshiva mentioned to the young man that he noticed how much he was enjoying his lunch. The young man answered that he loves salmon. The Rosh Yeshiva responded, "You don't *love* the salmon, young man, you love *eating* salmon. If you loved the salmon, you would have placed it in a fish tank, set up the perfect environment for the fish to flourish, and fed it every day."

"WE DON'T KNOW WHO TO FIX— OR WHETHER WE WANT TO"

In the case we have been discussing, both persons in the marriage show much more of the possessive or self-centered kind of "love" for the other than the deeply rooted respect, admiration, appreciation, and desire to give to the other, as should be present in a truly mature love for another.

Unfortunately, the husband mentioned above has been more focused on his need to feel loved by his wife than he has been on showing true understanding and appreciation of his wife's qualities and of her needs. His love is less rooted in a desire to give to his wife than it is in a drive to receive reassurance and unconditional acceptance from his wife. We can see this in the statement his wife made about him "being cheap and not wanting to spend money on vacations or anything fun." For years, she has been telling him one way to show his love in a manner that is meaningful to her, but he fails to respond to her need.

Similarly, she too is focused on her need to feel valued and appreciated for who she is, rather than as someone her husband "desires" and "smothers" with attention, which is clearly self-serving; he gives attention as a way to elicit her attention and appreciation. She pays lip service to her husband's qualities, but then proceeds as if those qualities are not the primary basis for her "love" for him.

Neither person elevates the other such that the desire to give of oneself to the other is paramount. Both persons in this marriage put on a "mask" in their attempt to express the recognition of the other person's qualities to each other, but the emotional energy is lacking. She repeatedly emphasizes her recognition that she is married to a truly good man, yet she brushes that aside in favor of the positive reinforcement she feels from all of her Facebook friends. Her husband is much better at telling his wife that he loves her than he is in conducting his relationship with her in a way that shows her that he respects her needs and wishes.

The second dimension of the contrast between Avraham and Iyov is rooted in Avraham's primary role in Jewish (and world) history. As described by Rabbi Wecker in the previous *d'var Torah*, Avraham's role can be described as "propagating and bequeathing to humanity an approach in serving Hashem." His gift to humanity is unsurpassed, and it certainly assures his importance over and above the impact Iyov has had.

We can draw a parallel between this dimension of Avraham's legacy and the opportunity that every husband and wife who are blessed with children have to bequeath to them, by their example—a way of showing genuine love. Parents have the opportunity to be role models whose genuine love for each other, as well as their love of Hashem, is unmistakably evident. Children always notice when one parent is placing the needs of the other parent above his or her own needs, and they learn that a parent who does this is one who loves their spouse in a way that exceeds their wish to have the other person love and need them. In our case, the couple did not have this kind of role model in their own parents' relationships. Perhaps not surprisingly, the three now-grown children from this marriage have each demonstrated early signs of relationship strains in their own marriages. Interestingly, while both parents certainly love their children and openly express a desire to conduct their lives in a way that benefits their children, their actual conduct in the marriage has impacted the children in ways that leave them less able to engage in mature, loving relationships.

In this clinical vignette, we have seen an approach in which both persons come to therapy wanting to "fix" the *other* person, to transform them into who they think they should be. This approach to resolving marital tensions cannot work. Such an approach is rooted in an immature notion of love, one that is self-centered and focused on expecting the other person in the relationship to take responsibility for meeting one's own needs. It is not rooted in a strong desire to give to the other person. The tensions which result trickle down to the kids, who learn to be self-centered in their own approach to the world and hence are likely to repeat a pattern of failed relationships, as well as experience adjustment issues of their own.

Let us now turn to an exploration of some of the issues we see in the children who are raised by parents whose self-focused approach to marriage interferes with their ability to see their child's needs clearly.

CHAPTER TWO

My Kid Is Broken, Please Fix Him

Rabbi Wecker

IN PARASHAS PINCHAS, THE TORAH STATES with regard to the Yom Tov of Sukkos:

> On the fifteenth day of the seventh month, there shall be a holy convocation for you; you shall not do work of labor; you shall celebrate a festival to Hashem for a seven-day period. You shall offer an olah-offering [completely burnt offering], a satisfying aroma to Hashem: thirteen young bulls, two rams, fourteen male lambs in their first year; they shall be unblemished.[20]

Rashi there notes that the bull-offerings of Sukkos number seventy, corresponding to the seventy nations, and they progressively decrease in number, i.e., each day fewer bulls are offered than the day before.

---

20   *Bamidbar* 29:12–13.

It is a sign of annihilation for the nations. And in the days of the Beis Hamikdash, the bulls would protect the nations from punishments.

The sheep correspond to Israel, who is called "a scattered lamb."[21] They are fixed, i.e., the number of sheep offered does not vary from day to day. The total number of sheep offered is ninety-eight, to neutralize the effects of the ninety-eight curses which are mentioned in *Devarim*.[22]

Sukkos is *zman simchasheinu*, a time for national rejoicing, a time when Hashem offers His love and His guarantee of protection to the Jewish People and the rest of humanity. Indeed, the Torah mandates with three positive commandments that we experience *simchah* (joyous celebration) on Sukkos.

In describing why the Jewish People might well be subjected to harsh punishments and the ninety-eight curses, the Torah says, "Because you did not serve Hashem your G-d with gladness and with goodness of heart, out of an abundance of everything."[23]

Rabbeinu Bachya comments: Their Divine service was devoid of *simchah*, and one is obligated to experience *simchah* when fulfilling the mitzvos; indeed, it is an additional mitzvah to experience *simchah* when fulfilling the mitzvos. One is rewarded separately for fulfilling mitzvos and doing so with *simchah*, and conversely one is censured separately on these two counts.

Rambam explains:[24] The *simchah* with which one should rejoice in the fulfillment of mitzvos and the love of Hashem Who commanded them is itself a great Divine service. Whoever holds back from this rejoicing is worthy of retribution, as it states, "Because you did not serve Hashem your G-d with gladness and with goodness of heart."[25]

One who fails to fulfill the mitzvos while experiencing a sense of *simchah* lacks far more than simply the mitzvah of fulfilling the mitzvos with *simchah*. This individual has demonstrated an attitudinal problem:

---

21 *Yirmiyahu* 50:17.
22 28:15–68.
23 *Devarim* 28:47.
24 *Hilchos Lulav* 8:15.
25 *Devarim* 28:47.

he/she does not regard the observance of mitzvos as important enough to be deserving of the experience of *simchah*. There is no appreciation of the unique opportunity presented by mitzvah observance and therefore a failure to bond effectively with Hashem. Such a tenuous connection to mitzvah observance simply cannot endure. That explains why this failure can justify the horrible consequence of having to endure the ninety-eight curses enumerated in *Devarim*.

Simchah is a critical component of one's overall service to G-d. Rav Moshe Feinstein[26] claimed that an entire generation of American Jewry was lost to traditional observance because they heard the message from their observant elders, either literally or subliminally, that "*Iz shver tzu zein a Yid*—It is difficult to be a Jew." He opined that, on the contrary, it is a great joy and honor to be an observant Jew, and that this message should be communicated effectively to the next generation.

SUMMARY

Simchah is a critical element in serving Hashem. One who serves Him without simchah manifests a profound lack of understanding of and commitment to mitzvah observance. Simchah is not simply an aspect of avodas Hashem; it is in many ways the defining element, the litmus test, of our hashkafah (outlook) toward our sacred Torah.

Dr. Weissman

Hi, I'm Diane and this is Jake. We're coming to you because we are concerned that our son, Kevin—actually he's Jake's son from his former marriage—is headed down a path of destruction, and we can't seem to do anything about it. He's been living with Jake and me for over a year now, after his mother finally admitted she couldn't handle him and sent him down to us. Jake has wanted Kevin to come live with us for a long time, but now that Kevin's with us, we can't control

---

26 Rosh Yeshiva in New York and foremost *posek* of his time. He lived from 1895 to 1986.

> him either. He's only seventeen, but he goes out drinking with his buddies most evenings, and won't come home until really late, hours after his curfew. He's even sneaking beer and liquor from our bar, and making it look like he didn't by putting some water back in the bottles. We're also terrified at the thought that he even might be tempted to "experiment" with other drugs. It's certainly hurting our relationship and making me very unhappy. We've been married for over five years now, and Jake has made it clear that he is very content with our relationship. Well, of course he is, because he controls everything, He refuses to combine our assets, income, etc. He likes to be in control of his money and everything. Anyway, I don't feel Jake pays me any real attention anymore. Look, even now he's just sitting there and letting me do all the talking, as if he's not the biggest part of the problem. He feels so guilty over his divorce from Kevin's mom; now he feels he has to make it up to Kevin, so he lets him get away with everything. Jake thinks that just having Kevin here with us will somehow magically make him change. He doesn't seem to believe in consequences for Kevin's out-of-control behavior or for the disrespect he shows us—especially me. All he ever does is "talk" to Kevin, asking him to follow the rules, and then sometimes he apologizes in case he was too "mean" to Kevin. So, Jake and I end up fighting all the time, while Kevin gets away with murder.

At this point in Diane's comments, I turned to Jake with a gesture, offering him an opening to respond.

> I knew she would turn this around making me the bad guy. Yeah, Kevin's got some problems, for sure, but we're working on them. Diane doesn't believe that I know Kevin better than she does nor that I know how to handle him. If she had her way she'd probably kick him out of the house, or she'd make it so miserable for him that he'd leave with nowhere to go—except

> to shack up with his buddies and get into even worse stuff, or try to get back with his mom, which, if you knew her you would agree, would be even worse. Diane always wants things her way, and she just doesn't want anything to interfere with her comfortable lifestyle. She should consider what Kevin's been through and make allowances. I just wish she'd leave him to me to take care of, instead of trying to control how I am with him as if she knows everything.

And so began an unusually challenging therapy process which morphed from a few couples' sessions to a greater number of individual sessions for Diane, as Jake grew more and more resistant to participating, and Kevin defied every "effort" on the part of his father and Diane to "insist" that he come to at least one session. Diane's individual sessions focused increasingly on her unhappiness with Jake, whose inability to follow through with any meaningful consequences for Kevin's behavioral and substance abuse issues left her feeling angry and unimportant. Jake even questioned her genuine concern for Kevin's wellbeing, as he continued to feel she was only pressuring him to take a "hard line" with Kevin in order to get Kevin out of her way so she could have Jake "all to herself." At the same time, her frustration at not receiving the kind of attention and appreciation she had always wanted from Jake left her increasingly depressed, to the point where it was beginning to impact her performance at work. Her self-esteem suffered, and as this was happening, her need for reassurance increased. Of course, this felt like still more pressure to Jake, who used that as an excuse to "focus" on Kevin. In reality, this meant trying to somehow contain some of Kevin's behaviors while making sure Kevin never got mad at him or threatened to "move out."

In this partial summary of an initial session, there are many intertangled issues which, together, form a complex dynamic of a family in serious distress, with the child, Kevin, playing the role of the initial "identified patient." Ostensibly, his unmanageable behaviors were the primary concern, but virtually within minutes of the beginning of the session, it became apparent that Jake and Diane were locked in a "tug of war" as Diane desperately tried to elicit Jake's love, attention, and appreciation, while Jake felt this as pressure and criticism of his way of dealing with his son (which even Jake admitted was not working).

In subsequent references to this particular case, we will address many of the specific issues, some which affect relationships between two or more people, while others reside more within a particular person in the family, and we will see how Torah principles and guidelines offer the healthy path to a resolution of these issues. At this point, let us focus on a "core" aspect of this sad family situation which is very much related to the words of Torah offered by Rabbi Wecker in the preceding *d'var Torah*.

Specifically, if one reflects on the clinical vignette outlining this family's distress, one will note, by conspicuous absence, any reference to joy in how the family members interact, pride in anyone's accomplishments, appreciation for the concern being expressed over Kevin's well-being, or gratitude for—or maybe even awareness of—the many blessings they share and that everyone seems to take for granted. As Rabbi Wecker's *d'var Torah* so beautifully described, just performing the mitzvos is certainly important, but performing them with *simchah*, with joy, at the good fortune of being in a position to perform the mitzvah, is the only route to true closeness with Hashem and to a truly loving relationship with our Creator.

In the same vein, many parents get caught up in just performing the duties of parenthood—earning a living, paying the bills, making sure homework is done, disciplining misbehavior, showing up at parent-teacher conferences or athletic events, and so on. Sadly, these "tasks" and "responsibilities" are often done without true joy and gratitude over the fact that we have people in our lives to whom we are able to give. If parenthood devolves into empty gestures done out of expectation, and not as a most precious opportunity and vehicle to show true love and become spiritually close to those we love, everything becomes a task, a chore, a responsibility. In the process, we lose countless opportunities to build deep and enduring bonds of love with those we care about most.

"HE THINKS JUST HAVING HIM LIVE WITH US WILL MAKE HIM BEHAVE"

Rabbi Wecker

The Torah records, "And Yitzchak loved Eisav '*ki tzayid b'fiv*,' but Rivkah loved Yaakov."[27] The phrase "*ki tzayid b'fiv*" can be interpreted in different ways:

- *Rashi*, in his first explanation, interprets it literally: "For Eisav's game was in his [Yitzchak's] mouth," i.e., Eisav provided his father Yitzchak with food.
- *Ibn Ezra* notes that Yitzchak had lost his great fortune and was now destitute. He was grateful to Eisav for providing him with his meals. (*Ibn Ezra* explains further that it is not unusual for a rich person, due to the force of circumstances, to be reduced to poverty.) According to this approach, Yitzchak felt an appropriate sense of gratitude to Eisav and as a result did not fully discern the latter's wickedness.
- *Rashi*'s second explanation is based on the Midrash: Yitzchak loved Eisav because "Eisav spoke to him deceptively." He pretended to be a G-d-fearing, mitzvos-observing person. He would ask Yitzchak halachic questions that would lead Yitzchak to believe that he was scrupulous in following Hashem's laws when in reality he was a heretic who had rejected the Torah lifestyle. Indeed, on the previous verse,[28] *Rashi* comments that Eisav asked his father whether one is obligated to take *maaser* (tithing) from salt and straw, both insincere questions meant to create an impression of his religiosity. According to this approach, Yitzchak was the victim of an elaborate and deliberate deception of Eisav, one that apparently was successful—for a time.
- A novel approach is suggested by Rav Yosef Chaim of Baghdad in his *sefer*, *Aderes Eliyahu*. He rejects the possibility that

---

27 *Bereishis* 25:28.
28 V. 27.

Yitzchak was oblivious to Eisav's shenanigans and evildoing. Instead, he posits that not only was Yitzchak was fully aware of Eisav's attempts to deceive him, but he noted further that Eisav was ashamed to exhibit any of his shortcomings in the presence of his father.[29] At the very least, Yitzchak reasoned, Eisav would not sin in his father's presence. Yitzchak hoped that perhaps their relationship would continue to develop, and Eisav could be subtly influenced to return to a Torah lifestyle. The alternative—confronting Eisav head-on over his duplicitous behavior—ran the real risk of ending any relationship between them and pushing Eisav even further away from Hashem.[30]

SUMMARY

There are times when one is well advised to allow the other party to set the tone in a relationship. Allowing the other to grow and mature spiritually is far more preferable to holding them to standards that may be objectively appropriate, but may nonetheless result in a severing of the bonds of friendship.

Dr. Weissman

Jake thinks that just having Kevin here with us will somehow magically make him change. He doesn't seem to believe in consequences for Kevin's out-of-control behavior or for the disrespect he shows us—especially me. All he ever does is "talk" to Kevin asking him to follow the rules…

---

29   See *Mishnah Berurah* 385:6: One who desecrates Shabbos in front of many people but is embarrassed to do so in front of a great *rav* is considered as one who desecrates Shabbos privately and not publicly, and is still considered an observant Jew in many regards.

30   Needless to add, one should be most hesitant before engaging in any form of deception, whether active or passive. Deception is almost always discouraged by the Torah and is to be utilized only in exceptional circumstances. One must be vigilant to avoid developing a negative *middah* (character trait) such as deception, and should consult a *rav* before deciding to act in such a manner.

This excerpt from the case just presented captures only one aspect of the complex dynamic playing itself out in this family in distress. Diane feels that the primary motivating factor behind Jake's parenting decision is his wish to assuage his guilt over the bitter divorce, many aspects of which Kevin witnessed as a child. Therefore, Jake has come to the belief that he "owes" Keven a place to live, and even more so, that he has a responsibility to shield him from conflict and tension. He never wants to risk Keven getting mad at him, which would threaten his view of himself as the father who is doing everything to "make it up" to his son. He is at least partially blind to the severity of his son's acting out and self-destructive behaviors.

Interestingly, one can see in this clinical situation examples of each of the three interpretations offered in the preceding *d'var Torah* to explain Yitzchak's relationship with Eisav. Here we see how Yitzchak seemed blind to his son's evil ways.

- The first interpretation Rabbi Wecker offers is based on one of *Rashi*'s two interpretations of the phrase *"ki tzayid b'fiv,"* namely the literal interpretation, implying that Yitzchak's appreciation for the food his son hunted and prepared for him fostered a special kind of mindset. In our case, the "food" which Jake receives from his son is his son not being angry with him, which satisfies Jake's "hunger" for approval from a son who might otherwise be very angry about what he experienced during his parents' divorce.
- The second interpretation offered follows directly from this, namely, that Yitzchak was vulnerable to his son's ability to be highly deceptive. Perhaps it was Yitzchak's strong desire to see his son grow in Torah that left him more vulnerable to Eisav's deceptive behaviors. In our case as well, Kevin's skill at deception and manipulation is effective with his father, whose guilt over the divorce fuels his intense desire to see his son as "doing well." Kevin repeatedly promises to follow the rules, but then threatens to leave and move in with one of his friends if the rules are enforced. He promises to make something of

himself by going to school, yet drops out soon after he begins community college because of not attending or doing any of the work. At times he expresses what appears to be appreciation for what he receives from Jake, but never misses an opportunity to point out some of Diane's shortcomings, which Kevin knows also bother his father.

- The third interpretation offered was that Yitzchak was aware of his son's deceptive behaviors, but Eisav behaved with deference and honor in the presence of his father. This left Yitzchak hopeful that as long as he does not drive his son away, he could foster more of these behaviors over time—due to the influence he would have over him as long as he remained within Yitzchak's domain. Similarly, Jake seems to hold onto the fantasy that as long as Kevin doesn't run away, over time he would make gradual changes and become a more mature and responsible young adult. Subsequent sessions with this family proved quite the opposite—while Jake allowed Kevin to return home after he served time in jail for dealing drugs, all the promises Kevin made to stay away from drugs and alcohol, to attend AA meetings, and to participate in therapy were never kept. In fact, I learned from another source that Kevin's acting out had actually *increased* in severity. He had been more openly defiant, such as drinking while at home and bringing friends into the house when Jake and Diane were gone, leaving obvious evidence of drug use.

Interestingly, Diane subsequently dropped out of therapy, I believe primarily because she didn't want to "face me" with the reality that her decision to go along with Jake's parenting decisions resulted in precisely the kind of disastrous result I had anticipated. As was the case with Yitzchak and Eisav, with Eisav continuing in his evil ways to the point of developing murderous intent directed toward his brother Yaakov, Kevin also demonstrated unchanged disregard for any reasonable expectations that would lead to a life of responsible, mature behavior.

"DO AS I SAY, NOT AS I DO"

Rabbi Wecker

The Torah notes that Yaakov wept when meeting Rachel for the first time.[31] *Rashi* explains that Yaakov reflected on the contrast between his situation and that of his grandfather Avraham's servant Eliezer. Eliezer came to find a wife for Yitzchak and happened upon Rachel's aunt, Rivkah. Eliezer showered Rivkah with many expensive gifts when the *shidduch* (arranged marriage) was made. Yaakov, on the other hand, arrived at his uncle Lavan's house destitute. Why was that so? Eisav's son Eliphaz was instructed by his father to pursue and kill his uncle, Yaakov. Eliphaz grew up studying Torah from his grandfather Yitzchak, and was thus unwilling to carry out his father's directive to kill Yaakov. Eliphaz asked Yaakov what he should do to fulfill his father's command. Yaakov suggested that Eliphaz take all of his possessions, since a poor person is in some ways considered like a dead person.[32] Thus, Eliphaz will have caused Yaakov's figurative "death."

Rav Chaim Shmuelevitz[33] noted how conflicted Eliphaz was. His *zaidy* (grandfather) and *rebbi*, Yitzchak Avinu, taught him how wrong it is to murder. On the other hand, the command of his father, Eisav, was important to him. His tutelage under Yitzchak brought him to the level of *ruach ha'kodesh* (a low level of prophecy),[34] while his desire to fulfill his evil father's wicked order caused him to rob Yaakov of all of his money and possessions and even his clothing, leaving him almost naked.[35] It is worth noting that murder falls into the category of *"mitzvos sichlios,"* commands that are morally repugnant under natural law.

It is amazing and frightening to realize how such sublime righteousness and debased evil can coexist in one human being. The Talmud states that Eliphaz was the ancestor of Amalek,[36] a nation dedicated to

---

31   *Bereishis* 29:11.
32   *Nedarim* 64a.
33   Rosh Yeshiva of the Mir Yeshiva. He lived from 1902 to 1979.
34   *Midrash Tanchuma, Parashas Vayeira* 38.
35   *Midrash Aggadah Bereishis* 28.
36   *Sanhedrin* 99b.

the forceful opposition to everything good and moral. Rav Shmuelevitz noted that it is precisely the moral relativism and the internal conflict of an Eliphaz that provided the fertile ground for the germination of the nation that personified all that is evil in the world.

The *Maharsha* notes that the Torah's effect on one's *neshamah* (soul) is comparable to the effect of a potent medication on the body.[37] If properly prescribed and administered, it can cure a serious illness; otherwise, it can pose a grave danger to the patient. We must turn to our *mesorah* (tradition) and our *rebbeim* (rabbis) for direction in the path of Torah. We must never allow ourselves to feel adrift and unanchored in our spiritual lives, for that can lead to spiritual disaster.

SUMMARY

Moral relativism and self-justification are dangerous pitfalls to spiritual growth. As Rav Yisrael Salanter put it, "On his way to perform a mitzvah, a person can destroy the entire world." Our intentions must of course be honorable, but our actions must likewise follow halachic guidelines precisely.

Dr. Weissman

The phrase "Do as I say, not as I do" has actually been used by many parents who believe that it reflects a valid way for parents to interact with their children. Of course, this could not be further from the truth. In fact, it is precisely this philosophy that often leads to the very defiant and maladaptive behaviors in children that have parents bringing them to therapy, hoping the therapist can "fix" their child. What they do not understand is that children learn to emulate the behavior they observe in their parents, regardless of what the parents tell them to do, especially if what they are telling the children contradicts their behavior.

For example:

- Almost all parents do not want their children to lie or to cheat. Yet, the very same parent who might be punishing his child for lying is often inclined to ask a family member to tell an

---

37   *Taanis* 7a.

unwanted caller "he's not home, can you call back later." This parent is actually *teaching* his child to lie.

- Similarly, the parent who tells his child, "Tell them you are eleven years old," when they are paying for amusement park tickets in order to qualify for the children's rate is not only teaching the child to lie, but also to cheat.

At the same time, due to the power and authority a parent possesses, including the right to implement discipline, a child is often caught in the middle between following what a parent tells him to do versus what the child learns to do through the parents' role-modeling. As we saw in the previous *d'var Torah*, Eliphaz was being told to do something by his father, Eisav, with the understanding that a child is supposed to respect the parent's wishes and do what the parent tells him to do. At the same time, he was told to do something that was completely opposed to what he learned from his grandfather, Yitzchak, who not only taught him the laws of proper conduct, but who also exemplified in his behavior the character structure of a person who truly *lives* the laws he is teaching. We see that this is a far more powerful influence over the child's behavior, as Eliphaz is extremely careful to not violate the core value he learned from his grandfather, namely, not to murder, because his grandfather lived by it. He even turned to his uncle—the very man he was supposed to kill—for advice regarding respecting his father's wishes in some way, which also involves an important Torah law.

Fortunately, Eliphaz was blessed with the grandfather of such high moral character that his influence predominated over the hypocritical and evil request made by his father. Eliphaz did not kill his uncle Yaakov, but "merely" robbed him in order to fulfill Eisav's evil command.

In the case we have been discussing, Kevin is unfortunately left with the worst of both possible situations, as he does not have a role model whose behavior he can strive to emulate, nor does he have a parent who is able to properly teach him basic rules of conduct and proper respect. It behooves all of us, especially those of us who are blessed with children and the opportunity to raise them with essential core values, to follow the maxim, "whatever you want for your children you must BE IT, and not simply pay lip service TO it." If you don't want your children to smoke, don't smoke. If you want your children to obey traffic laws, obey traffic laws. If you don't want your children to use improper language, don't use improper language. If you don't want your children to engage in gossip (*lashon ha'ra*), don't gossip. If you want your child to grow up to be a loving husband or wife, you must be a loving husband or wife.

"WE DON'T SEE EYE TO EYE ON MOST THINGS, INCLUDING HOW TO PARENT"

Rabbi Wecker

The Torah discusses the *ben sorer u'moreh*, the rebellious son.[38] In summary, a male within three months of becoming a bar mitzvah who steals and eats a prescribed amount of meat and drinks a prescribed amount of wine is subject to the death penalty. The Talmud questions why a young man who has committed these acts (which are not capital crimes) is to be executed.[39] It answers: The Torah foresees the direction this young man is headed. He will soon squander his father's property, and need to find other means to support his hedonistic lifestyle. He will rob people and commit some capital act in the process. The Torah prefers that he die innocent of those crimes rather than wait for him to actually commit them and die guilty.

The question arises: How can the Torah be so certain that this person is destined to follow this downward trajectory?

Ibn Ezra claims that this child is a heretic and wants only to enjoy decadent physical pleasures. Rav Chaim Shmuelevitz suggests that it is his total engagement with hedonism that paves the way for his downfall. Such single-minded dedication to self-indulgence means that he is destined for self-ruin.

Ramban submits that he has dishonored his parents who have scolded him to no avail, and he has sunk to a level of gluttony and drunkenness

---

38 *Devarim* 21:18–21.
39 *Sanhedrin* 69a.

that demonstrates that he is unconcerned with spirituality. Sadly, this profile leads only to further self-degradation.

Ibn Ezra (cited above) offers another perspective. He notes that this *parashah* immediately follows that of the *ishah yefas to'ar*, a beautiful captive non-Jewish woman. He suggests that as the mother of this wayward young man, the captive non-Jewish woman had no desire to adopt Jewish mores and morality. Her lack of commitment to Torah values was reflected by her son becoming a *ben sorer u'moreh*.

Perhaps the most powerful external influence on our lives is our mother. The influence of an evil mother represents a hurdle that is almost impossible to overcome.

Rav Shmuelevitz explains a comment of Talmud Yerushalmi[40] as meaning that in the end, this wayward son will forget his Torah knowledge.[41] The Rosh Yeshiva notes that as long as some Torah knowledge remains, there is hope for a change to the better. The merit of that Torah can inspire the most jaundiced *neshamah* to do *teshuvah* (repentance). When that last flicker of Torah and *kedushah* (holiness) is extinguished, however, there remains little hope that he will return to the path of our holy and sacred Torah.

My *rebbi*, Rav Dovid Feinstein, *shlita*, notes an apparent inconsistency in the Torah's narrative:

- Initially, the *ben sorer u'moreh* is described as one who did not listen "to the voice of his father and the voice of his mother."[42] The implication is that the parents did not speak with one voice, and that there was some disagreement about how to instruct the child.
- Later on, when the parents file a complaint with the *beis din* (Jewish court), they state that "he does not listen to our voice."[43] Here, the implication is that both parents are in agreement with regard to their son's direction.

---

40   Ibid., 8:7.
41   The *Pnei Moshe* offers a different explanation.
42   *Devarim* 21:18.
43   Ibid. 21:20.

My *rebbi* inferred that parents are much more likely to be successful in raising a son who accepts their teachings when they work in unison. Although the *ben sorer u'moreh*'s parents appear to have followed that course when appealing to the *beis din*, unfortunately the damage done by their earlier conflict has already had a negative impact on their child.

SUMMARY

We are all faced with temptations that would steer us away from living a Torah lifestyle. Hedonism can be a powerful allure. Our baser instincts urge us to put aside the restrictive lifestyle of our faith and instead enjoy the physical. The Torah can, of course, strengthen our resolve to do what is right, and it is from our role models—parents, rabbis, teachers, and others—that we both learn about and observe healthy behaviors. Mixed messages from these authority figures can muddy the waters and complicate our decision-making processes.

Dr. Weissman

I can't even believe the way Jake thinks about handling Kevin. I know that setting strong rules, along with appropriate discipline, is necessary. This kid needs to have boundaries—and consequences if he violates those boundaries. Jake thinks that that sort of thing only makes the kid mad and drives him away. It really irritates me because Jake is very rigid and demanding regarding what he expects from me. He's really OCD; everything has to be perfect, just so, and G-d forbid if I don't comply with every picayune thing he wants me to do, he either throws a fit or withdraws and pouts. This kid is going to drive us apart. Meanwhile, nothing changes with Kevin. I know he's still drinking even though his dad doesn't want to believe it, and I'm pretty sure he has taken some pills from my medicine cabinet. When I mention that to Jake he accuses me of taking too many pills myself, or of counting wrong. The whole thing is unbelievable. And the worst thing is that he is so adamant in insisting that his way of dealing with Kevin is the right way,

> even though he admits we are not seeing behavior change the way we had hoped. He just wants me to hang in there and go along with his lackadaisical attitude about parenting. It's all so unfair. If I ask anything of him and he's too busy, he makes me feel that I'm greedy or insensitive for making demands on him. I'm not sure where this marriage is headed, but it isn't looking too good.

Not surprisingly, Diane's words as quoted above go directly to the core of the kind of parenting the Torah specifically challenges us to avoid. It is the clearest example of parents who do not speak with one voice. This couple's opinions are so divergent that nothing of substance can happen in the form of a plan to deal with their child. While it looks like Kevin, originally the identified patient, is the "bad guy" in this family situation, it's more accurate to consider him a victim of a situation in which the two adult authority figures in his life cannot agree on anything, with the result that he is falling through the cracks.

Another piece of information regarding this case needs to be mentioned here, as it relates to the part of Rabbi Wecker's *d'var Torah* which focuses on the consequences of having a mother who is immoral or in some other way entirely inadequate. This appears to be the case with Kevin's biological mother, whom both Jake and Diane describe as a seriously disturbed woman who only thinks about her own needs and who was never sufficiently available for Kevin during the period of time when she had primary custody, or for that matter, during the time she and Jake were married. Indeed, it was she who decided to let Kevin live with his father instead of trying to have Kevin stay with her. Perhaps the only area in which Jake and Diane actually agree is in their shared dislike for Kevin's biological mother. Therefore, on at least two scores, Kevin is again the loser:

First, his biological mother appears to have lived a life focused on herself, and therefore is a person who did not know how to bond with her child.

Second, Jake and Diane reinforce Kevin's negative view of his biological mother, leaving him even more emotionally stranded. Although this does not excuse his behavior, it is understandable that he would turn to some form of comfort he can control, such as drugs and alcohol. Even though he has had legal difficulties because of this, he does not have the maturity nor the support of a caring, loving family that are necessary to overcome his maladaptive behaviors.

The only truly effective parenting is rooted in Torah values:

- Whatever you want for your child, you must *"be it."*
- Both parents must speak with one voice.
- Never discipline a child when you are angry. (A parent who is angry might discipline a child as a way to vent their anger, rather than taking the time to gain emotional composure and then decide the best approach to teach the child proper behavior. We will have much more to say on this topic later in the book.)
- Effective parenting involves much more than just having your kid at home and hoping that he will somehow absorb what he needs to become a good, functioning adult. A child needs to see the love and respect his parents have for one another.
- Ultimately, each child needs parents who fully understand why in Hebrew the word for love, *ahavah*, literally means "to give."

CHAPTER THREE

No One in Our Family Gets Along

Dr. Weissman

DR. WEISSMAN: *Hi, I'm Dr. Weissman. I understand that you have been working with another therapist, Ms. Safire, for almost a year now, and you all agreed that somehow you are stuck and not making any progress. I'm sure you've covered a lot of territory in all that time, but I would like to suggest that we begin as if I know nothing about your situation except that you have been in marital therapy and are now beginning with a new therapist to see if a different approach, with a male therapist, might help. Please let me know what's been going on.*

Jennifer: Well, okay, I'll start. Our marital problems started approximately three-and-a-half years ago during my pregnancy with our second child, Casey. He was born with some medical issues—most significantly, impaired hearing. While all this was going on, George, who is in the army, was deployed for a brief two-week mission to Bahrain. Shortly after his return, a soldier killed himself and George was assigned to the CACO team, an acronym for the "casualty assessment" division, where each officer is assigned to a case in which some trauma has occurred. He was assigned to work with the family of the soldier who committed suicide, and his superior officer told George that he had to meet every request and need of the family, putting them first, even over and above his other duties and his own family. This meant that he was gone almost all of the time after Casey was born, and at about the same time I got laid off from my job working from home for a financial service company. Because of the responsibility of caring for the new baby, as well as my older daughter, I decided not to pursue other work. I found myself becoming more and more resentful that George had become almost completely disengaged from the day-to-day activities of the household, including any direct care of our new son.

Dr. Weissman: Well, George, Jennifer is certainly expressing a lot of strong feelings, all pointing to her being very upset with you. I imagine you may not agree with some of her harsh criticism.

George: Yeah, I see it differently. And as always, she leaves out a lot of stuff—anything to do with where she might be a part of the problem. She's constantly nagging me, and that drives me crazy. Sometimes our arguments erupt into a yelling match.

Jennifer: What do you mean "sometimes"? You're always the one to yell and scream at me, and you say very hateful things, like saying you want a divorce. Right after Casey was born, you began to express doubt about whether you wanted to stay married. It's gotten so bad that we can't talk about anything anymore without it turning into an argument. I feel like I'm walking on eggshells all the time, never knowing when you're going to explode because I didn't do something exactly the way you wanted me to do it or because I forgot to do something. You just don't see that I'm always busy with the kids and can't get things done the way you want them done. Why don't you try to stay at home and take care of the kids for a day, and see how much you can get done?

Dr. Weissman: I can see how tense things get between you guys, as it is obvious that right here in this session, tempers are flaring and communication is breaking down. Sometimes when communication breaks down, it affects a variety of other important areas in the marriage. Are there any other specific issues which seem to cause conflict or tension?

Rabbi Wecker

The Torah narrates, "Pinchas, son of Elazar, son of Aharon HaKohen, saw what had happened, and he arose from the midst of the community, and he took a spear in his hand."[44]

Pinchas is portrayed in two different ways that seem to be mutually exclusive:

- On the one hand, Pinchas is described as the ultimate *kana'i*, the zealous defender of the faith, who killed Zimri, the *nasi* (prince) of the tribe of Shimon[45] for having sinned with the Midianite princess, Kazbi.
- On the other hand, he is simultaneously identified as "the grandson of Aharon," the latter serving as the model of *"ohev shalom v'rodef shalom,"* loving peace and seeking peace.[46]

How can we reconcile these two seemingly contradictory descriptions?

Rav Chaim Shmuelevitz explains by pointing out that a similar dichotomy, or contrast, is apparent in the feelings of Avraham Avinu for his firstborn son, Yishmael:

- When instructed to drive Yishmael out from his home, Avraham provided him with nothing but a loaf of bread and a

---

44 *Bamidbar* 25:7.
45 See *Sanhedrin* 82b, where he is identified as Shlumiel ben Tzurishadai.
46 *Avos* 1:12.

jug of water. Yishmael was dangerously ill at that time. *Rashi* explains that Avraham did not provide Yishmael with gold and silver (or any other items) because he loathed him for being a *rasha*, a wicked person.[47]

- Yet, when G-d commanded Avraham to "take your son and offer him as a *korban* (a sacrifice)," he replied, "I have two sons." G-d elaborated, "Your only son." Avraham responded, "Both are the only sons of their respective mothers." G-d continued, "Whom you love." Avraham responded that he did not differentiate between his two sons in his love for them. Thus, Avraham told G-d, who knew the thoughts of Avraham's heart, and before whom nothing is concealed, that his love for Yishmael equaled his love for Yitzchak. It is clear, then, that his love for Yishmael was genuine.

How then do we understand the conflicted feelings of Avraham for Yishmael?

The explanation is that Avraham's emotions were governed by right and wrong, and he was able to channel and direct different emotions, even toward the same person, even toward his own son. We think of love and hate as being mutually exclusive emotions.

Unlike many of us, Avraham controlled his emotions and was not controlled by them. His feelings were not a reflection of any personal bias. He could simultaneously feel genuine paternal love for Yishmael and animosity and revulsion at his waywardness.

Moreover, the Torah states that it was *only* because Avraham loved Yishmael so deeply that he permitted himself to chastise him so severely.

One who metes out punishment to another person must *first* be filled with love and compassion for his fellow. Only then is he permitted to act with *kana'us* (zealousness). Pinchas was so motivated, and he could punish Zimri *precisely* because he was the "grandson of Aharon HaKohen," who was the model of "loving and seeking peace."

We are taught: Resh Lakish said, "When the enemy nations entered the Beis Hamikdash to destroy it, they found the *keruvim*, the angelic

---

47 *Bereishis* 21:11.

youths whose statues stood in the *Kodesh Hakodashim*, in the inner sanctum, in embrace."[48] The *Maharsha* questions this, noting that the embrace of the *keruvim* bespoke G-d's love for, and closeness with, the Jewish People.[49] How could it be that at the very moment of the destruction of the Beis Hamikdash, of the murder of millions of Jews, and the exile of those who had escaped immediate death, the *keruvim* would embrace?

The answer is that *since* Jewry was being severely punished by G-d, there *had* to be this expression of utter Divine closeness and love. Only at such a time of intimate embrace could G-d destroy the Temple and exile His chosen people.

A few *parshiyos* earlier, the Torah describes the mystical process through which a person contaminated with *tum'as meis* (impurity caused by direct contact with a deceased person) can be *metahar* (purified). The process involved using the ashes of the *parah adumah* (the red heifer). The mitzvah of *parah adumah* is an enigma, since it produces two seemingly contradictory results:

- It purifies one who contracted *tum'as meis*.
- It is also *metamei* (contaminates) the *Kohen* who prepares it.

Zos chukas haTorah—in its description of this mitzvah, the Torah implies that it is somehow a paradigm for the entire Torah. How does *parah adumah* serve as a standard for the entire Torah?

Rav Moshe Feinstein explains that the apparent self-contradiction serves as a model for all mitzvos. Every character trait, if utilized appropriately, can be used to serve G-d, yet, if it is misused, it can be detrimental and harmful. For example, one must be generous to others but stingy with himself. One who is naturally generous will not respect his funds or those of others. The Torah admonishes him: Do not steal from or defraud people even for the sake of *tzedakah*. On the other extreme, one who appreciates the value of money will not steal or defraud others, but he will not spend his own funds for *tzedakah*, something which is also improper. We are

---

48   *Yoma* 54b.
49   *Bava Basra* 99a.

therefore exhorted to abide by the golden mean, i.e., the mitzvos dictated by the Torah. Through doing so, we resolve all character trait conflicts, and we are able to live with inner harmony and peace.

Rav Yosef Dov Soloveitchik notes further that although this approach of dichotomy, of oscillation between two extremes, is "exceptionally complex, rigorous, and tortuous," it is absolutely necessary because it reflects our complex reality. Our holy Torah addresses the complexities of both the human psyche and of our multifaceted existence. It guides us through the minefields we encounter throughout life, and provides us with what Rav Henoch Leibowitz called "the elixir of life."

SUMMARY

Great tzaddikim are not controlled by their emotions; on the contrary, they are in control of their emotions and model the Torah ideal in their thoughts and actions. Love and concern for others is assuredly a Torah ideal. Avraham, for example, deeply loved his son Yishmael but strongly disapproved of his choice to rebel against the Torah and expressed it and acted on it where appropriate. Yet that strong disapproval did not diminish his love for Yishmael. Furthermore, even when Hashem deemed it necessary to destroy the Beis Hamikdash, He simultaneously expressed His love for us and reassured us of His commitment to the eternity of the Jewish People and our ultimate redemption.

The Torah models appropriate behaviors for us, and through following its guidelines faithfully we will achieve, b'ezras Hashem, that elusive inner harmony and equilibrium that we all desire.

"WE DON'T EVEN SPEND TIME TOGETHER LIKE WE USED TO"

Dr. Weissman

George: Just like you said, Doc, our communication breakdown affects everything. We can't make any decisions without arguing. I think because we argue so much we don't know how to be close to each other at all, or for that matter, even how to talk!

> *There's hardly any affection in our marriage anymore. We're always fighting about whose job it is to do something. I try to help out with the two little kids upstairs while she takes care of getting stuff cleaned up after we eat and then trying to get the two older kids to bed—but she always yells at me saying I'm not helping her enough. Meanwhile, she's home all day, and I come home to a messy house—toys all over the place, laundry just sitting there, dishes in the sink—and she's sitting around playing with her iPad or iPhone, while the kids are doing their own thing. It seems she pays more attention to those gadgets than she does to any of us. Even when we have a little bit of time at night to watch TV, she's not really watching with me; she's on Facebook or doing something with her phone that makes me feel that she doesn't care if I'm around or not. So why not talk about divorce? As far as I can tell, she's the one that seems uninterested in being married.*

George went on to describe his high level of stress at home in his relationship with Jennifer. He said, "The way she comes across, I feel like I've always got to walk on eggshells. She is constantly critical of me and treats me in ways that make me feel like a child." Presently, his mother is living with them because her husband suddenly asked for a divorce. Her presence does not appear to be a significant stressor, primarily because Jennifer gets along very well with his mother, and she helps with the kids.

While George stated that he feels Jennifer is always critical of him, Jennifer countered that he is overly sensitive and takes offense at everything: "It doesn't matter how I say something to him, he always gets upset and at times angry. After that, he just withdraws and shuts down." George went on to say that he doesn't feel that she loves him in the way a wife should love a husband: "I feel like I'm the janitor, the maid, and the gardener—everything but a husband." He added that they do not go out together, never go to movies, do not even sit and watch TV together, and that affection has disappeared from their marriage.

During the course of this discussion about the stressors in their marital relationship, Jennifer made reference to what she believes to be a "terrible childhood" that George experienced, which may account for some of his difficulties in nurturing the marital relationship. Interestingly, this is the only time she expressed any hint of empathy for her husband or a reason to explain some of his behavior. She said that he was always teased and at times bullied by children in the neighborhood. George added that his father was always a very prominent person in their hometown, serving as a popular athletic coach and also on the city council. His personality is such that he was always "butting into everyone else's business." Apparently, many families in the community resented this. For example, George's father would show up at an athletic event insisting on offering a critique of the prior performance of other children based on his "knowledge" of their weaknesses. He was aware of these weaknesses because he had videotaped the children and analyzed the tape. Many parents, as well as the children themselves, resented this.

George's parents divorced, and he has been estranged from his father since his father remarried. Jennifer feels that this history of a highly strained relationship with his father is a significant contributing factor affecting his ability to comfortably assume the role of father and husband.

Both Jennifer and George stated that their discussions get nowhere, and they realize that they have a severe breakdown in communication. They acknowledged that they both end up saying very hurtful things to the other, usually by demeaning the other person. They agreed that they are willing to try one more attempt at therapy with the goal of trying to address these communication issues. They also want to address underlying issues regarding both of their abilities to express their own needs and feelings and to be responsive to the other's needs and feelings.

This was the first meeting that I had with Jennifer and George, and it was clear that they were presenting with a myriad of interconnected issues that result in a family which is always close to a state of chaos. In complex situations such as this, it is important to find a place to start where both persons feel that what they have to say counts, that their feelings are important, and that the other person in the relationship wants to understand their feelings. None of this can begin to take place before there are basic ground rules of communication to guide interactions. Jennifer and George have virtually no ground rules for communication, nothing to guide how they speak to each other, much less try to communicate deep feelings to each other. Thus, the starting place is in helping them learn that there are proper ways to talk to each other as well as ways that are unacceptable—ways that never work and therefore need to be identified and then abandoned. I chose to use a tool I often use in situations such as this in which communication is "broken," namely, what I refer to as "role-reversal therapeutic letters," in which each person writes a letter as if they were the other person, expressing that person's feelings to the best of their ability.

Before picking up this case to share with the reader how a step-by-step approach can build a healthy relationship, let us see what the Torah has to tell us. The Torah is infinitely rich in giving us rules for living that can be learned from the way our forefathers conducted their lives, as well as from the commandments themselves.

Rabbi Wecker

The Torah records Eisav's sale of his birthright to his younger twin brother, Yaakov.[50] Later on, when their mother, Rivkah, discovered that their father, Yitzchak, had informed Eisav of his desire to bestow his *berachos* upon him, Rivkah convinced Yaakov that the *berachos* were rightfully his and that he must impersonate his brother to ensure that he receive them. (Yitzchak was blind at this time). After the scheme was carried out to its conclusion, Eisav came to his father to receive the *berachos*. When he discovered what Yaakov had perpetrated, Eisav "cried greatly and bitterly."[51]

The Midrash states: "Yaakov caused Eisav to cry out. When were his [Yaakov's] descendants punished for his act? In the Purim story, where we learn that Mordechai 'cried a long and bitter cry'[52] after hearing of Haman's plans to annihilate Jewry."[53] (Mordechai was a descendant of Yaakov and Haman was a descendant of Eisav).

---

50 *Bereishis* 25:29–32.
51 Ibid. 27:34.
52 *Esther* 4:1.
53 *Yalkut Shimoni*, par. 115.

Rav Reuvain Grozovsky[54] questions this statement of the Midrash. Yaakov acted as he did on the command of his mother, Rivkah, who was a prophetess, and one is obligated to follow the directives of a *navi*. Furthermore, had Yaakov not acted so, the Jewish People would not have become Hashem's chosen people, and that was Hashem's plan and His purpose for creating the entire universe. In light of these facts, what was Yaakov to do? He simply had no choice but to act as he did! Why did he deserve "punishment" for doing what he had to do?

Rav Grozovsky answers by affirming that the pain of a person is never neutralized until it is redressed. A human being, created in the image of Hashem, was created to enjoy life,[55] albeit a redeemed life achieved through mitzvah observance. Causing pain to another human being runs counter to Hashem's goals and must be accounted for. Even though hundreds of years separated the actions of Yaakov Avinu from the Purim story, the hurt was not forgotten, and the pain caused to Eisav had to be expiated.

Rav Chaim Shmuelevitz comments on the sad tale of Kamtza and Bar Kamtza. The Talmud relates the following story:[56] A certain man had a friend named Kamtza and an arch-enemy named Bar Kamtza. The man prepared a feast and sent his servant to invite Kamtza. The servant mistakenly invited his nemesis, Bar Kamtza, instead. Upon seeing Bar Kamtza at his feast, the host ordered Bar Kamtza to leave. Bar Kamtza pleaded with him to be allowed to stay, even offering to pay for the entire affair. His pleas were rejected and he was unceremoniously ejected from the premises. Bar Kamtza plotted his revenge against the entire Jewish People, claiming that no one among the assembled rose to his defense. He was, unfortunately, successful. The Talmud concludes the narrative by quoting the words of Rabbi Elazar: "Come and reflect on the severity of shaming one's fellow. Hashem supported Bar Kamtza's nefarious scheme, and as a result His Beis Hamikdash was destroyed."

---

54   Rosh Yeshiva at the Kamenetz Yeshiva in Europe and at Yeshivas Torah Vodaas in New York. He lived from 1886 to 1958.
55   See *Rabbeinu Bachya, Bereishis* 2:15.
56   *Gittin* 55b–57a.

Rav Shmuelevitz notes that Bar Kamtza was a man of vile character, a man who stooped so low as to slander his own people to the Roman emperor. His actions were responsible for the *churban Beis Hamikdash* and the wholesale death and destruction that came in its wake. Yet, his dignity, too, was sacred. Indeed, his humiliation was the cause of these calamities.

Thus far, we have noted two examples of the destructive effects of causing pain and hurt to another human being. The opposite is also true: an altruistic act can bring the *geulah* (redemption). Rav Yehuda Zev Segal, the Manchester Rosh Yeshiva, notes that the Midrash records Rachel's plea to Hashem at the time of the *churban Beis Hamikdash*.[57] Earlier, prayers from Avraham, Yitzchak, Yaakov, and Moshe for the newly exiled Jews were rejected by Hashem. Then Rachel pleaded to Hashem, "You, Hashem, know that Your servant Yaakov felt an extraordinary love for me. He worked for seven years in order to marry me. When the time came for us to wed, my father schemed to put my sister Leah in my place. I found out about the deception and was quite upset. I informed Yaakov of it, and we agreed upon a signal with which he could identify me and foil my father's plot. Later, I reexamined my plan and abandoned it out of pity for Leah. I simply could not bear the thought of her shame on my account. Now," Rachel concluded, "if I, who am but a mortal human, was not jealous of my sister, then certainly You, who are Eternal and have no competitors, can forgive Your people for worshipping idols, which are worthless and meaningless, and save Jewry from destruction!" Hashem's mercy was aroused, and He replied, "Because of you, Rachel, the Jewish People will return to Eretz Yisrael (with the coming of Mashiach)."

Thus, we see that one noble, selfless act, performed long ago in antiquity, is never forgotten and will be cause of our *geulah*, *b'meheirah v'yameinu*, amen.

SUMMARY

Shaming or causing pain to a human being runs counter to Hashem's desire and can have catastrophic consequences, on both the micro and the macro level. By contrast, acting altruistically can bring benefits that will last an

---

57   *Eichah Rabbah*, introduction, end of section 24.

eternity. Rachel's selfless act will, according to the Midrash, bring about our ultimate redemption.

Dr. Weissman

George and Jennifer returned for their second session with the role-reversal therapeutic letters I asked them to write:

- The essence of the letter that George wrote *as if he were Jennifer* focused on what he knows to be her concern about them not working together as a team, her distress when he loses his temper, her hurt and anger when he is hypercritical of her, and her frustration with his being distant and uninvolved in the day-to-day responsibilities of running a household.
- The letter Jennifer wrote *as if she were George* conveyed that she believes he is primarily driven by his belief that she is not happy with him, that she doesn't respect or appreciate all that he does, and that she doesn't show enough affection.

Interestingly, their letters suggest that they *do* know each other's feelings and perspectives on what is wrong with their marriage. Yet, when they try to discuss their feelings, especially when there is already some tension between them, it is as if that knowledge of the other person's point of view evaporates. Even more so, their communication regresses to the point where they both strike out precisely at the point of the other person's vulnerability.

The manner of communication exhibited by both George and Jennifer might be seen as reflecting the antithesis of the wisdom so beautifully conveyed in Rabbi Wecker's previous *d'var Torah*. It appears that when engaged in a "discussion" neither of them is thinking about "loving the other as they love themselves." Nor are they thinking about "not doing to the other what you would not have them do to you." And certainly, they are not thinking about what they each can do to be as supportive and helpful and sensitive as possible in dealing with their spouse.

During the course of the session, I focused on helping them see how they have been treating each other and how harsh and hurtful their words are when they argue. I pointed out how they are not considering how they would like to be treated and using that as a guiding philosophy in determining how they treat the other.

It was not difficult to convey this perspective; their therapeutic letters "proved" that they do understand each other, in contrast with how they actually behave when they argue. However, awareness of this insight is not always sufficient to bring about meaningful change in how they communicate and interact with each other. It is often the case that focusing attention on a specific way for them to work more cooperatively together can leave both persons with the feeling that they are being supported. Therefore, it was necessary to find a specific "challenge" they could embrace together which would directly address an important need or feeling pertinent to each person's distress in the marriage, and thereby reinforce the importance of giving to the other. In our initial session, we saw that a main source of conflict involves George's OCD tendencies, which seem to dominate his interactions with her and the children. Jennifer also expressed her own need to be organized and structured, but her need for organization is not at the same level of intensity as his OCD issues, in that he gets genuinely distressed and unable to tolerate small "messes" or things out of order, while she simply prefers to be able to do things in her way. For example, his compulsion to put things away without telling her, such that she can't find them herself, is an obstacle to her being effective in how she tries to manage the household.

At the end of the session I again suggested some specific homework, namely, that they sit down and come up with his "OCD list," and then discuss her main concerns about structure and running the household (her "OCD list"). Next, they should try to work out compromises and ways to deal with their differences in ways which reduce conflict and tension. Thus, they would both be engaged in a "project" of identifying differences in their respective needs regarding the enormous challenge they face in running a household harmoniously and in peace. They were both very responsive to this suggestion and expressed positive anticipation about the prospect of resolving some of the chronic tension between them.

Rabbi Wecker

According to one view (*Tashbatz Hakatan*), all the customs of the *chassan* (groom) and the *kallah* (bride) on their wedding day are derived from the events of *Matan Torah*, the revelation at Sinai when allegorically Hashem married His beloved bride, Knesses Yisrael, the Jewish People.

Other rabbis (*Kol Bo* and other Rishonim[58]) claim that many of the customs of the wedding are derived from acts that Hashem performed for Adam and Chavah on their wedding day (soon after their creation).

What is the connection between these formative events, the creation of the universe and *Matan Torah*?

Rashi[59] notes that the Torah added the definite article (the Hebrew letter *hei*) only to the sixth day of *Brias Ha'olam* at the conclusion of the work of creation. This was done in order to teach that Hashem stipulated that the act of creation was dependent upon Jewry accepting the Torah many generations later. If Jewry would fail to accept the Torah then, the entire universe would return to its initial state of void and emptiness.

Is there a stronger connection between these two pivotal events of creation and revelation?

The Midrash[60] notes that at *Matan Torah* "no bird twittered, no fowl flew, no ox brayed, none of the *Ofanim* stirred a wing, the *Serafim* did not recite their praise of Hashem, 'Holy, Holy,' the sea did not roar, the creatures spoke not, the whole world was hushed into breathless silence and the voice went forth, 'I am Hashem your G-d.'"[61]

Why was all of creation silenced precisely when the Torah was given?

- Perhaps so no one could be misled into imagining that there was more than One G-d, *chas v'shalom*.
- Another explanation, offered by Rav Elya Meir Bloch, Rosh Yeshiva of the Telshe Yeshiva, is that before *Matan Torah*, mitzvah

---

58   Earlier Torah authorities who lived approximately in the eleventh to fifteenth centuries.
59   *Bereishis* 1:31.
60   *Shemos Rabbah* 29:9.
61   *Shemos* 20:1.

observance was somewhat optional: Yaakov married two sisters, Moshe's father Amram married his aunt, and so on; both acts that were later prohibited by the Torah. In specific circumstances, before the Torah was actually given, even known mitzvos could be overruled temporarily to accomplish a specific goal. At *Matan Torah*, however, all of creation was in a state of suspended animation while the spiritual composition of the universe was re-created with this different property. From that point and onward, mitzvah observance simply could never be suspended. Hashem decreed that all of creation must be silent to symbolize this change in the process of spiritual growth, this re-creation of the permissible means that lead to spirituality. From *Matan Torah* onward, halachah must be followed if one is to serve G-d.

Perhaps, the lesson to be learned from this discussion is that the institution of Jewish marriage rests on three pillars:

1. ***Bereishis***: Marriage represents a new beginning, akin to the very creation of the universe itself. The *chassan* and *kallah* will develop, deepen, and broaden their relationship.
2. ***Matan Torah***: The commitment of the *chassan* and the *kallah* to the Torah and their determination to faithfully follow and transmit our sacred *mesorah* (religious heritage) to the next generation of Jews should form the bedrock of their goals and aspirations.
3. **Potential**: Just as the goal of *Brias Ha'olam* was achieved only at *Matan Torah*, so too the *chassan* and *kallah* should recognize both their own and their spouse's great potential and work together to actualize them.

The Talmud[62] states that Rabbah bar bar Chanah quoted Rabbi Yochanan: "Making successful *shidduchim* is as difficult as the parting of Yam Suf." *Maharal*, in his Talmud commentary, notes that both the parting of Yam Suf and successful *shidduchim* contradict the natural

---

62 *Sotah* 2a.

order of things. Splitting the sea and causing a break in the flow of water is obviously an unnatural act. Similarly, it is unnatural for two independent and autonomous human beings, each with his/her separate personal temperament and aspirations, to unite as husband and wife and become one unit (literally, "one flesh").[63] The *Maharal* concludes that although this union may be "unnatural" from a physical standpoint, it can be accomplished in a spiritual sense through a fusion of the two *neshamos*. The successful *chassan* and *kallah* look beyond the constraints of physicality to develop their relationship. Rav Yosef Dov Soloveitchik expressed this idea when he noted that "in some mysterious way, the 'I's' find solace in each other." A new metaphysical creation, "husband X and wife Y," is created with a successful *shidduch*. Their relationship becomes even further solidified with the birth of their progeny.

The Talmud states:[64] "In the west (Eretz Yisrael), when a man marries a woman, he is asked, '*Matza* or *motzei*?' *Mutza*[65] refers to 'One who has found (*matza*) a wife has found good,' and *motzei*[66] refers to 'And I find more bitter than death the woman who ensnares.'" (Many *mefarshim* note that the *chassan* is not expected to respond to the questioner, since doing so could involve speaking *lashon ha'ra*. Instead, he is asked to reflect on these ideas for his own benefit and edification.)

The Gra explains the use of the two terms in the following way. Human nature is such that we tend to pay little notice when things are going well. On the other hand, we tend to obsess with negative experiences. *Mutza* refers to the habitual and routine. We take for granted a wonderful spouse and do not express our thanks to him/her and Hashem as often as we should. *Motzei*, on the other hand, is written in the present tense. A bitter experience is remembered, and more so, is often replayed in our minds as something ongoing.

The lesson is, of course, self-evident. We need to be mindful of the good, and express our gratitude often to both our spouse and to

---

63 As per *Bereishis* 2:24.
64 *Berachos* 8a and *Yevamos* 63b.
65 *Mishlei* 18:22.
66 *Koheles* 7:26.

Hashem for the bounty that we enjoy. On the other hand, we need to reinforce our trust in Hashem when we experience the bitter, and stoically accept His judgment, all the while realizing that He has only the best intentions for us.

The critical importance of wedding a noble spouse and the sometimes tragic consequences of marrying a dishonorable one, are starkly delineated in the story of Korach's rebellion against Moshe.[67] Ohn ben Peles is listed as one of the conspirators at the beginning of the narrative[68] but he escaped the punishment meted out to his fellow plotters. The Talmud[69] says that his wife said to him, "You gain nothing from your involvement in his revolt. If Korach wins, you will retain the same secondary role you have now that Moshe is in charge." With his agreement, she arranged for him to be uncommunicative, and prevented his accomplices from contacting him, thus ensuring his survival.

The Midrash records that Ohn's wife even successfully pleaded with Hashem to spare his life when the moment of retribution arrived.[70]

The Midrash (ibid.) records further that Michal bas Shaul was one of three women who saved their husbands from death. The *Midrash Socher Tov* elaborates:[71] Michal saved her husband, David (later to be crowned king) from the hands of her father, Shaul. Thus, were it not for the heroic actions of Michal in leading David out of the palace via a path that bypassed Shaul, David would have been killed. As we know, Mashiach will be a descendant of David (and may we merit his arrival speedily in our time). Thus, Michal's role guaranteed the survival of both her husband David and his progeny, including the Mashiach. There can be no greater testament to the value of a noble wife.

Korach, on the other hand, had the exact opposite experience.[72] His wife incited him, convincing him that Moshe sought to disrespect him and disenfranchise him, all this to deprive him of the honor that was his due.

---

67 *Bamidbar* chap. 16.
68 Ibid., 16:1.
69 *Sanhedrin* 109b–110a.
70 *Midrash Hagadol, Bamidbar* 16:32.
71 59:1.
72 *Sanhedrin* 109b–110a.

SUMMARY

Marriage represents a new beginning, akin to the very creation of the universe itself. The chassan and kallah will develop, deepen, and broaden their relationship.

The commitment of the chassan and kallah to the Torah and their determination to faithfully follow and transmit our sacred mesorah to the next generation of Jews should form the bedrock of their goals and aspirations.

Just as the goal of Brias Ha'olam was achieved only at Matan Torah, so too the chassan and kallah should recognize both their own and their spouse's great potential and work together to actualize them.

The successful chassan and kallah look beyond the constraints of physicality to develop their relationship. Rav Yosef Dov Soloveitchik expressed this idea when he noted that "in some mysterious way, the 'I's' find solace in each other."

We need to be mindful of the good, and often express our gratitude to both our spouse and to Hashem for the bounty that we enjoy. On the other hand, we need to reinforce our trust in Hashem when we experience the bitter, and stoically accept His judgment, all the while realizing that He has only the best intentions for us.

A noble spouse can support his/her spouse, and a dishonorable one can sometimes cause much harm.

"HIS MOM MOVED HERE TO HELP, AND NOW SHE'S THE PROBLEM"

Dr. Weissman

George and Jennifer continued to come reliably to their weekly therapy session, despite their frustration when minor steps of progress were typically followed by a regression to their old patterns of not listening to each other. At times they would not even try to make the changes that would show concern about the other person's distress. In one particular session, Jennifer opened by saying that she had been especially overwhelmed lately. She explained that George's mother moved there the previous spring with the hope that she would be able to help out with the kids in the morning, the busiest time for Jennifer, but instead she had taken a part-time job that prevents her from being available at those hours. As result, Jennifer feels overwhelmed, and she reported that she and George often work at cross-purposes. We saw that George can be extremely defensive about his mother, and at other times he "explodes with anger" when confronting his mother about her neglect of their rules for handling the children or her intrusive critical comments about the way in which they raise the children. I chose to address this by making reference to Steven Covey's well-known book, *The Seven Habits of Highly Effective People*, in which he says that "sometimes we're too busy chopping down the tree to stop and sharpen the saw!" Covey explains that "in doing a task, we generally become so engrossed, we tend to neglect the basic tools." He also interprets "sharpening the ax" as referring to taking care of your most important asset—*you*. This concept therefore refers to both how one goes about dealing with life's challenges as well as making sure that you are "at your best," both physically and emotionally (spiritually). I shared this famous quotation and then explained how they were neglecting to "sharpen their tools" in their approach to their challenges. We discussed how they needed to take the time to plan how they were going to handle challenging situations. One area of particular concern is actually something they agree on—that his mother does not take the fact that both of their young children have food allergies seriously, and sometimes she will be out with the children without taking the EpiPen with her or will not even make sure they are not exposed to any of the ingredients in food that trigger their allergic reactions. We discussed ways for them to approach his mother in a more effective manner—rather than the way in which George would simply confront his mother in anger. I suggested that they find an opportunity to invite his mother to participate in a three-way discussion about how they can help her become more aware of and responsive to the specific needs their children have. Most of the session focused on the importance of them finding time to discuss ways for them to know when it is necessary and appropriate to step back from the tense situation in order to "huddle" and come up with a plan.

Of particular significance in this situation regarding his mother's impact on the marriage and family is the fact that they allow his mother to cause a "split" in their relationship. We will go into more detail in the next clinical vignette about the importance of placing the marital bond over and above other relationships, a point which is emphasized many times in the Torah. At this point, however, the main goal was trying to help them come up with a plan to address some specific issues which stem from the disruptive role that his mother plays in the family dynamic.

Rabbi Wecker

Rav Avraham Yeshaya Karelitz, known popularly as the *Chazon Ish*,[73] offers an important perspective on our current spiritual condition, which can also be seen in our conduct with others. He notes that the halachah forbids us from interacting with and supporting fellow Jews who are not committed to Torah observance.[74] He comments that those *halachos* were in force only in ancient times, when Hashem's presence was clearly perceived, when obvious miracles were a frequent occurrence, and *tzaddikim* enjoyed heavenly support that was manifest to all. In that milieu, heresy represented an intolerable negative influence that had to be opposed. Divine punishment for tolerance of such sacrilege might include enemy invasion, drought, or famine.

Nowadays, however, when Hashem hides His governance of the world and of our lives, *emunah* has been greatly weakened, and it is counterproductive to take extreme measures against non-believers. To do so would serve to drive people further away from our Torah (*chas v'shalom*). Instead, we should endeavor to influence others to return to Hashem with "bands of love."[75]

In a way that parallels this commentary on our current spiritual condition, we can see that taking a position on any particular issue cannot be at the expense of rejecting or demeaning others. If this approach is relevant to the issue of possible heresy and improper *hashkafos*, then how much more so is it relevant to the area of interpersonal relationships where

---

73 He lived from 1878 to 1953.
74 *Yoreh Deah, Hilchos Shechitah* 2:16.
75 *Hoshea* 11:4.

one's ego can easily lead him/her down a destructive path and negatively impact the lives of his/her loved ones. We should strive to conduct our relationships with the understanding and acceptance that the other person comes to his position based on his own personal life experience, and therefore one cannot stand in judgement of the other person. In a comment clearly meant to discourage acting this way, Rav Yisrael Meir HaCohen Kagan,[76] the sainted Chafetz Chaim, advised against engaging in *machlokes* (dispute) unless one is both physically stronger and less of a *tzaddik* than his opponent. I have a *mesorah* from a number of my *rebbeim* that conflict and discord are rarely an appropriate option. The approach of *machlokes* is far more likely to lead to further discord, causing *lashon ha'ra*, hatred, and other severe sins, than it is to bring about a positive result. Whether dealing with family, friends (present and former), associates, or others, a pleasant and positive manner is the preferred approach.

SUMMARY

Just as in the current spiritual climate in which a Jew is rarely guilty of intentional and premeditated heresy, in our day-to-day relationships we should not treat others, especially our loved ones, in a condemning, judgmental manner, as if their point of view is "heresy." Just as the Torah strictures on positive relationships with non-observant Jews are suspended, we should strive to "suspend" our own critical judgement of others. In fact, one is rarely justified in acting aggressively against anyone. Such actions rarely produce positive outcomes, and often only exacerbate issues and result in negative outcomes.

"SHE PUTS EVERYTHING ELSE BEFORE ME"

Dr. Weissman

One of the most frequent underlying issues in couples struggling with their marriage is some version of one or both persons feeling that the marital bond is relegated to a lower priority than other individuals or

---

[76] He lived from 1838 to 1933.

interests. Often this involves a particular "other" with whom one person in the marriage has such a strong bond that the spouse feels "displaced." This might be a parent, the children, one's job, a particular friend, or even an inanimate object like a cell phone, TV, tablet, computer, etc. Often, one is not aware that he or she is actually doing this—relegating the marriage to a lower priority than someone (or something) else. At other times, the individual is acutely aware that he or she is doing this, but with some rationalization or justification in his or her mind as to why this is the proper way to proceed. The case we have been following is replete with examples of how both persons registered the same complaint regarding the marriage being less important than something else pulling their spouse's attention away from the relationship.

> *George was seen individually today because the babysitting arrangements fell through and his mother could not fill in; therefore, Jennifer had to return home instead of meeting him here. Nonetheless, we had a very productive discussion in which he described in some detail his perception of how Jennifer controls their communication and undermines his efforts to connect with her. He states that she is always on her iPad on the sofa when he comes home, and she watches TV or is otherwise involved in her social networking most evenings, while he takes care of much of the household responsibilities. He again repeated that he feels like the servant in the house. When I talked with him about finding time to talk with Jennifer about the relationship, he indicated that he has thought about it but wasn't able to actually initiate it. He complained that whenever they are together, they have to talk about the children's schedules, upcoming events, etc. He then said that there are certain TV shows that they would miss if they turned the TV off and started to talk. Of course, I challenged him about what is really important, but he persisted in saying that it is primarily Jennifer who would have a hard time redirecting her attention to a conversation with him. I believe he offered a very helpful formulation regarding the dynamics of the relationship, which from his point of view is more adversarial*

than cooperative, with her always having to be the one who "wins," wanting to be the one who is always "right." As a result, when he tries to begin a conversation, she turns it around to some complaint about him. He feels the situation is hopeless, but I challenged him on this by pointing out that our main focus in therapy is to help change this type of communication. He agreed with this, and affirmed that in our next session it would be very important for him to be fully open with her regarding all of these observations, many of which he has never shared with her.

Rabbi Wecker

Rav Yosef Dov Soloveitchik noted that the Torah and Midrash provide us with extensive information about our *Avos* (patriarchs), but the role of our *Imahos* (matriarchs) is relatively obscure. In fact, Sarah was an equal and indispensable partner of Avraham in the covenant and in the propagation of the faith.

Rashi comments: "'The souls they had made in Haran.' Avraham converted the men, and Sarah converted the women, and the Torah accounts it as if they had made them."[77] As a result of their efforts, tens of thousands became part of the household of Avraham. Only by acting in concert and through complementing each other's efforts could Avraham and Sarah together have achieved this degree of success and *kiddush Hashem*.

"I will remember My covenant with Yaakov as well as My covenant with Yitzchak, and also My covenant with Avraham I will remember." How do we know that the matriarchs were also part of the covenant? The word "*es*" (a grammatical term in Hebrew that has no English language equivalent) is written three times in this *pasuk*. The inclusion of the matriarchs is derived from the repetition of the word, "*es*."[78] Avraham's role is given more prominence because it was he who was active in public life.

The Torah records that when three angels, disguised as nomads wandering the desert and who were eagerly invited by Avraham to share a

---

77   *Bereishis* 12:5.
78   *Yalkut Shimoni, Vayikra* 675.

meal, asked Avraham, "Where is your wife, Sarah?" he replied, "Here in the tent."[79] *Rashi* explains that the angels knew where our mother Sarah was, but they asked this question in order to call attention to her modesty and so to endear her all the more to her husband.

In some matters of a personal and family nature, Sarah's spiritual sensitivity was greater than Avraham's. When her husband hesitated about sending away Hagar and Yishmael because of Yishmael's harmful influence on Yitzchak, G-d said to Avraham: "All that Sarah says to you listen to her voice."[80] *Rashi* clarifies that we may infer that Avraham was inferior to Sarah in respect to prophecy.

> *And Avraham said to G-d: "May it be granted that Yishmael live before You." G-d replied: "But your wife Sarah will bear you a son, and you will call him Yitzchak, and I will keep My covenant with him as an everlasting treaty, for his descendants after him."*[81]

G-d explained that His covenant cannot be realized without Yitzchak. Why? Because Yitzchak is the son of Sarah. Yitzchak will emerge from Avraham and Sarah, but Yishmael is only from Avraham; there can be no covenant without Sarah.

The Torah does not discuss much of Avraham's life after Sarah's death. Although he outlived her by many years, he realized at some point that his mission as the father of the covenantal community was concluded, and that from that point, all he had to do was to act out the last part of the drama and walk off the covenantal stage, making room for someone else to succeed him.

The great *baal mussar* Rav Eliyahu Eliezer Dessler notes that the key to a successful marriage is that each spouse should always strive to make the other happy.[82] But when one spouse constantly makes demands of the other, happiness will not evade them.

In addition, both spouses should daven to Hashem for the success

---

79 *Bereishis* 18:9.
80 Ibid., 21:12.
81 Ibid., 17:18–19.
82 *Michtav Me'Eliyahu* I, p. 39.

of their marriage. *Rabbeinu Bachya* notes in his *sefer*, *Kad HaKemach*, "To be successful, a marriage needs G-d's help. This lesson is mentioned three times in our Tanach."

Indeed, Rav Chaim Shmuelevitz writes that even though we know and believe that G-d orchestrates every aspect of our lives, that sense is perceived more clearly in the area of choosing a spouse and marriage.

SUMMARY

Avraham and Sarah were successful in their outreach efforts to bring people closer to Hashem because they worked in unison and complemented each other's efforts. It is only as a result of their joint efforts that Avraham and Sarah became, respectively, the patriarch and matriarch of the Jewish People. Working independently, neither one would have been able to reach that level of success.

A healthy marriage results only when the husband sees his goal as striving to make his wife happy, and vice versa.

We need to be cognizant of the role played by G-d in orchestrating the events that lead to the marriage of two people and pray to Him for the continued health of the marriage.

CHAPTER FOUR

They Tell Me I Have an Anger Problem

Dr. Weissman

WITHOUT QUESTION, ONE OF THE MOST frequent presenting problems in the therapist's office involves anger management.

- Occasionally a therapist receives a call from someone who recognizes that they have a problem with anger and on their own initiative is seeking help with the recognition that their method of handling anger has never worked, and frequently has gotten them into some form of trouble.
- At other times, the therapist may receive a call from someone who is a "mandatory referral," meaning that their employer referred them to therapy as a condition for their continued employment, once again due to problems the individual has had dealing with anger, in this case in the work setting. Such individuals may still be highly defensive, disagreeing with the referral and arriving in an active state of denial, while others have "owned" the fact that they have an anger problem and are

willing and cooperative as we begin to understand and address the problem.
- Most of the time, especially when working with married couples and families, the issue of anger comes up in connection with one or more family members having difficulty with a particular person's anger issues, especially as that person's anger impacts the rest of the family. Perhaps surprisingly, it is also one of the most easily denied issues, not only within the person who has the anger problem, who generally sees his or her anger as entirely justified, but also by the spouse or other family members, usually because of their fear of the angry person's reaction if they were to confront the issue.

It is this third category, where some denial is involved, that usually constitutes some of the most substantive issues in the entire therapy process. Therefore, our focus will be on addressing anger issues which surface in the context of marital or family therapy.

Sometimes it is possible to address how one person's anger impacts all other members of the family in the very first session. For many, the very fact of being "in therapy," and being able to talk to a therapist who, hopefully, conveys both empathy and compassion, allows the spouse or other family member to finally "take the risk" and talk about what up to this point had been the "forbidden subject." However, it is also not unusual for this issue to be minimized or totally denied for a number of therapy sessions until some event occurs that forces a discussion of this issue. Regardless of the manner in which the issue of anger management comes up in the therapy office, finding a way to help the person accept the fact of having this problem is the first major challenge. This challenge often involves helping the spouse who has been the "victim" of the other person's anger to find a "voice," or even to help that person recognize some of their own behaviors which have contributed to or enabled the problem. For the moment, we will continue to explore how this issue manifests itself in Jennifer and George's marriage. Later, we will also see some clinical vignettes from a few different cases which clearly illustrate the extent to which serious anger issues can be denied and avoided despite having an obviously devastating impact of the marriage and family.

> We just came back from our vacation in Philadelphia. We go there at least every other year—we have some old friends who live there—and this time we had a pretty enjoyable time. However, things really started to go downhill starting with the day before we were getting ready to leave Philadelphia and come home. There was escalating tension as George became increasingly frustrated. He struggles when things do not go his way, to the point where he threw a real "doozy" of a temper tantrum. While yelling at all of us as we were packing up, he literally threw a bag of cookies across the room when I made a comment reminding him of the diet he had proudly proclaimed just a few days ago. He was getting even angrier, this time almost screaming at everyone when we couldn't quite keep up with the plan for our departure time—things just took longer than we anticipated. Then he "closed down" and wouldn't talk for most of the ride home, but it was obvious he was fuming inside. Of course, by the time we arrived home six hours later I didn't want anything to do with him, so I put the kids to bed and then picked up my iPad so I could at least connect with some of my friends who understand my feelings and really care about me. As usual, it wasn't until later that evening, when we were about to go to bed, that he apologized for losing his temper. I appreciate that, but he shouldn't expect me to be all "warm and fuzzy" with him, as if I hadn't been treated horribly by him for most of the day.

In George and Jennifer's therapy, we had previously touched on the issue of his angry reactions, but only in the context of his frequent critical comments and passive-aggressive withdrawal from her when he is frustrated. The incident summarized above was the first time the extent and severity of his angry outbursts was so apparent. Most the session focused on how easily he is aroused to anger with minimal frustrations, and we saw how the primary work for him at this time is to learn how to modulate that reaction. Yet, we also see that Jennifer can contribute to tensions in the marriage when she shuts down and disengages in her own passive-aggressive behavior, rather than pointing out her concerns about his escalating anger as it begins to manifest. Indeed, her first "go-to place" when she is passive-aggressively distancing herself from him is to immerse herself in her cell phone or iPad—precisely the behavior which she knows is particularly irritating to him. By the end of this particular session, they were very receptive to my suggestion that they come up with a specific "plan" as to how they can give each other feedback as soon as one of them appears to be showing the kind of inappropriate reactions which were evident in the incident summarized above.

At the next session, Jennifer and George were able to come up with a combined list of ground rules for communication, containing ten specific points as follows: cell phones off during any serious discussion, make sure to state that a particular conversation is important, arrange set times for especially important conversations, acknowledge that a conversation is taking place and therefore a response is indicated, no sarcasm or exaggeration, state clearly if input from the other person is being requested, no escalating volume or change in tone, no threats of divorce or leaving, avoid any "trigger comments to push the other person's buttons," take turns talking, and use timeouts when helpful or appropriate. We went into detail discussing some of these points, but our main focus was on a persistent feeling that George has that she doesn't really want to talk with him and is not interested in what he has to say. She assured him that most of the time she is interested, although there are times when he goes on and on about a topic that's either above her head or overly detailed, which has the effect of making her feel less inclined to engage. Therefore, we discussed how he needs to be more sensitive as to whether the person he is talking with is fully engaged with the topic he is discussing, and to be more sensitive to the situation at that time in order to assess the kind of communications which is appropriate. At the same time, she needs to be aware that her ADD tendencies (which she claims make it difficult for her to focus) can feel like disinterest to him. We focused on a specific approach, namely, that when George wants to talk to Jennifer about something of such a nature that he needs to know she is engaged, he might consider briefly touching her hand or some other signal to make sure she knows that at least for that initial part of the conversation, he needs to know that she is invested and engaged. They were both very receptive to trying to implement these communication tools.

Rabbi Wecker

Sefer Shmuel I opens with the story of Chanah, the righteous woman. She was childless and came to the Mishkan to pray to Hashem that she have children. She prayed with *kavanah*; her lips moved as she recited the words of her prayer, but no one around her heard her voice.[83] Eli, the *Kohen Gadol* and leader of Jewry, observed her actions and thought she was intoxicated—one may not pray in such a state. He reproved her for davening in such circumstances, but she replied that she was quite sober, and was simply praying fervently to Hashem to end her troubles.

The *Navi* records: "And Eli answered: 'Go in peace, and may the G-d of Yisrael grant your request.'"[84] The Talmud records the teaching of Rabbi Eliezer: "From this *pasuk* we learn that one who falsely suspects an innocent person must mollify him; and not only that, but he must bless him in addition."[85] The *Pnei Yehoshua* questions how this *pasuk* proves that one must mollify the person he mistakenly suspected. Perhaps all that is necessary is to bless him, as is indicated in the *pasuk*? He answers that the wording of the *pasuk* appears out of proper order: Eli should first bless her that Hashem should respond favorably to her requests, and only thereafter wish that she "go in peace." He therefore concludes that here "go in peace" means that we (Eli and Chanah) should be reconciled, and only thereafter did he bless her that Hashem should grant her wishes.

---

83 Her example became the model for davening *Shemoneh Esrei*, see *Berachos* 31a.
84 *Shmuel I* 1:17.
85 *Berachos* 31b.

According to the *Midrash Toras Kohanim*, it is a Torah mitzvah to give the benefit of the doubt to another observant Jew (unless one has specific grounds to suspect the individual of wrongdoing).[86] The *Rambam* includes this sin of mistakenly suspecting another of wrongdoing in the list of sins for which one generally doesn't repent.[87] The offenders tend to rationalize their failure to do *teshuvah* by claiming that no harm had been done. They fail to realize that the mere thought of mistakenly suspecting someone is itself sinful.

Rav Yisrael Salanter is quoted as having noted that when he first began to study *mussar* (Jewish moral, ethical, and spiritual perfection), he became upset with the world but not himself.[88] Later on, he became upset with himself as well. Finally, he remained upset with himself but judged the world favorably. He realized that while he saw himself as needing continued efforts to reach his spiritual potential, he was obligated to judge other people charitably with regard to their development.

It is axiomatic that human relationships are based on trust. Violation of that trust can easily snowball into a full-fledged conflict. If this is true of all human association, how much more so is it true of close familial relationships where issues are often magnified.

SUMMARY

It is a Torah obligation to judge another person favorably and to give him/her the benefit of the doubt, unless one has specific grounds to suspect otherwise. Since human relationships are based upon trust, the opportunity to fulfill this mitzvah occurs often, especially at home, at work, and with peers. At times, we may take liberties with family, friends, and co-workers, and judge them negatively without giving them the benefit of the doubt. Familiarity may breed contempt. The Torah warns us to treat everyone, from close friend to occasional acquaintance, favorably and generously.

---

86 19:39, quoted by *Rashi, Vayikra* 19:15.
87 *Hilchos Teshuvah* 4:4.
88 *Ohr Hamussar*, vol. 1, p. 55.

"WE CAN'T EVEN TALK ABOUT THIS ISSUE WITHOUT ARGUING"

Dr. Weissman

We are temporarily going to leave Jennifer and George to discuss another interesting case which clearly illustrates how denial of a serious anger management issue can result in a virtual "explosion" in the relationship once an event occurs that makes the issue impossible to avoid. It is important to note that anger management issues always are the result of more "deeply buried" issues related to a need to control. This may manifest itself in many forms, such as road rage (wanting to control how everyone drives), bullying others, physical aggression in response to frustration, dominating others in relationships, verbal abuse in response to frustrations, excessively harsh discipline of the children, etc. As we shall see in subsequent sections in this chapter as well as later in the book, "control" is a central concept that offers the clearest, most direct "link" between the therapy office and the Torah view of character development and healthy relationships.

Given the importance of anger management issues and the "need to control" in driving both character development and how we conduct ourselves in all of our relationships, let us examine a case which captures and conveys the complex interplay between the "presenting problem" and underlying anger and control issues. We will see a detailed account of how this particular case unfolded, including excerpts adapted from clinical notes, showing how anger management issues which have been denied or avoided surface at unexpected times in ways which reveal multiple "layers" of various "intertwined" relationship issues. As you will see, this interesting case unfolded in somewhat distinct "phases," and Rabbi Wecker will offer his Torah thoughts at each phase. Let's begin.

Courtney and Roy were my patients in marital therapy approximately a year ago. Courtney is a forty-six-year-old Caucasian female who comes to therapy accompanied by her husband, Roy. Her chief complaint is depression, anxiety, and anger at her husband, as well as concern about the escalating stress on the marriage. Roy agreed to accompany her because of his recognition of how strained their marriage is, noting that their frequent arguments interfere with their ability to experience a fulfilling relationship. He also acknowledged his own struggle with depression which he also linked to the marital tensions.

Courtney began the initial session by saying, "I think I made the appointment because we cannot talk about a particular issue; we get too upset, we can only argue about it, and never really talk about it." When I asked what issue she was referring to, she explained that this is the second marriage for both of them, and together they have a twenty-one-year-old son, Cole. Courtney has a daughter (Katie) in her late twenties from her first marriage and Roy has a son (Ted) in his early twenties from his first marriage.

Courtney went on to say that when they got married they moved into Roy's house, and that throughout the years she has tried to talk with him about putting her name on the house. Additionally, they have a great deal of struggle trying to agree upon how to write their wills. Roy is adamant about not negotiating any of these issues. His will states that the house goes to his two children exclusively, therefore excluding Courtney from inheriting part of the house. He also refuses to discuss putting Courtney's name on the house. Courtney is even willing to pay him in order to be named on the deed, as she has money from the sale of the house she lived in before divorcing her former husband. She and her ex-husband have been responsible for financing their daughter's college education. Additionally, partly because of their inability to even discuss their conflicts regarding their wills and ownership of the house, Courtney has used money she had received as part of the divorce settlement to buy her own rental property, spending $30,000 for the down payment, leaving her $40,000 which she described as a "safety cushion" for her in case the need arises—possibly if the marriage fails. He feels that she is financially secure—she works as a full-time teacher in a local public high school. He added that she even made the decision to buy the rental property without consulting him. Courtney feels that he does not recognize or appreciate her contribution to the marriage over the past years, as evidenced by Roy trying to prevent her from ownership in the financial resources she believes should be considered as money and property they both own as a married couple. She feels that the fact that she has contributed financially during the years to the running of the household—including purchasing most of the groceries—she has "earned" her part ownership in what she considers to be shared marital assets. Roy responded by saying that he does value her and her contribution to the marriage, but he strongly resists any change in the deed to the house, citing the expense of having to renegotiate a mortgage, the fees involved in changing the deed, etc. She believes these are all excuses, and that, in fact, he does not trust her or want her to have part ownership in the house or other marital assets. Interestingly, the situation is complicated because Roy is a Certified Public Accountant (CPA), and therefore verbally overpowers her with his "expertise" about the best way to handle money. As a schoolteacher, she has a more limited income, and therefore she is concerned about her future and the future of her children. Every time they have tried to discuss these issues they immediately begin arguing and soon become totally paralyzed in terms of making any progress in resolving these issues.

Both Roy and Courtney confirm that they do love each other very much and want the marriage to work. In many other respects they feel they have a good marriage, such as enjoying time together, especially when on vacation, enjoying times when they feel close to each other, and feeling that they have a good division of labor that makes day-to-day interactions involving running the household largely free of conflict. It is only when they get to this financial issue that tensions escalate to the point where they spend significant amounts of time not talking to each other, leaving both of them feeling depressed and unfulfilled. They said they are coming to therapy to find help in communicating about this issue, and more generally, to improve the way that they handle conflicts when they occur in their relationship.

Rabbi Wecker

In Jewish law and tradition, a core focus is placed on the sanctity and centrality of the Jewish home and marriage. We can begin with the wedding ceremony itself. An important part of the Jewish wedding ceremony is the preparation and reading of the *kesubah* document. The *kesubah* document obligates the husband (or his estate) to provide a financial settlement to his wife in the event of either divorce or his death. The standard amount specified in the *kesubah* is two hundred *zuz* and two hundred *zekukim* of silver. Although some *poskim* claim that the *kesubah* is a Torah obligation, the consensus is that it is an enactment of the Sages.[89] There is a *machlokes* about the value of the items listed. Rav Moshe Feinstein states that the value of two hundred *zekukim* of silver equals one hundred pounds of silver.[90] He suggests further[91] that the *kesubah* amount must be large enough to deter a divorce, regardless of the current value of silver. Rav Shlomo Zalman Auerbach[92] notes that the *kesubah* also provides the wife with a sense of security and trust in the permanence of the marriage.[93]

Further, a millennium ago, Rabbeinu Gershom enacted a *cherem* (ban) on polygamy, and mandated that halachic divorce may occur only with the mutual consent of both the husband and the wife. The *Rama*, whose comments on the *Shulchan Aruch* are generally binding on Ashkenazic Jewry, notes that since Rabbeinu Gershom's decree changed the dynamic of the halachic divorce (which was heretofore usually the exclusive prerogative of the husband) to one in which the wife had a decisive voice, "It is possible to be lenient and not write a *kesubah* at all, but this is not the accepted custom and one should not change it."[94] The consensus of *mefarshim* is that the *kesubah* must be maintained as part of the halachic wedding ceremony. Rav Moshe notes that "a married woman should not be without her *kesubah* for even a short time."[95]

He records further that in the present day, many *rabbanim* have not examined the issue of the exact value of the *kesubah* since now women

---

89 See *Shalmei Simchah* by Rav Shlomo Zalman Auerbach, p. 242.
90 *Igros Moshe, Even Ha'ezer* 4:91–92.
91 Ibid., *Yoreh Deah* 1:189.
92 He lived from 1910 to 1995.
93 *Shalmei Simchah*, pp. 242–243.
94 *Even Ha'ezer* 66:3.
95 *Igros Moshe, Orach Chaim* 5 9:3.

have greater bargaining power in the halachic divorce process.[96] These women are in a position to insist on financial settlements to their liking, and their husbands must be prepared to appease them. Given their strong bargaining position, the *kesubah* settlement has little practical ramification.[97]

Although our *chachamim* made provisions for sustenance for the wife in the event of a divorce, a divorce should be utilized only as a last resort. It is far preferable for a husband and wife to address the challenges to their marriage, and put forth an honest effort together to resolve them. Rav Shimshon Raphael Hirsch[98] describes the ideal relationship between a husband and wife. He writes as follows:

> *In order to become a true ezer (companion) it would be preferable if she possessed qualities that are different from his. This will serve to stimulate their marriage, as they will be better equipped to solve together the tasks and challenges which lie ahead. Her position is totally equal to that of her husband; she stands kenegdo (his equal): husband and wife, wife and husband—one complements the other.*[99]

He also writes:[100]

> *The chachamim expect a husband to treat his wife with the most tender consideration, love, and respect. The first man called his wife, "the mother of all living things," that is why a husband should give in to his partner and not cause her grief.*[101]

---

96 Ibid., *Even Ha'ezer* 4:91.
97 See the next *teshuvah*, however, where he notes that the value of the *kesubah* is still relevant today in certain unique circumstances.
98 He lived from 1808 to 1888.
99 *Collected Writings*, vol. 8, p. 56.
100 *Collected Writings*, vol. 8, p.133.
101 *Kesuvos* 61a.

---------- SUMMARY ----------

Although our great rabbanim made provisions for divorce and a woman's maintenance, one must strive to make his/her marriage work. Focus on the many benefits that accrue to both husband and wife, and make a concerted effort to discard any insults, whether real or perceived.

Dr. Weissman

Given the fact that the specific reason Courtney and Roy came to therapy was to help them work through what they describe as a complete inability to even discuss critical aspects of their financial arrangement, at the end of the initial session I suggested that a productive way to begin the process of breaking the "logjam" would be to suggest the same homework I used in my work with George and Jennifer, namely to write "role-reversal therapeutic letters." I explained that this homework involves each of them writing a letter as if they were the other person, trying the best they can to express what that person would say about the marriage, their communication, their financial arrangement, etc. I explained that this would offer a mechanism to get to the underlying issues as well as improving their ability to understand the other person's point of view as they attempt to work through areas of conflict. They were both very receptive to this suggestion, and they agreed to bring their "therapeutic letters" to our next session.

We began the next session by taking the time for both of them to read the role-reversal therapeutic letters they had written based on our homework from last session. Roy's letter, in which he tried to convey what he believed to be Courtney's deepest feelings about their marital conflicts, actually was quite extraordinarily empathic and seemed to reflect the depth of her feelings of hurt and rejection, and the importance she places on having some significant financial stake in the marriage for the sake of her own self-esteem as well as wanting her daughter to be taken care of. As he was reading his letter Courtney was able to reach over and touch his arm, in what appeared to be a sincere gesture of appreciation for his level of understanding of her feelings. She read her letter, which was more cryptic (to reflect his style of communicating), but she also did a good job expressing the reasons why Roy does not feel it is necessary or appropriate to put her name on the mortgage to the house or change their wills such that all three children are guaranteed an equal share in the shared marital assets. Her letter explained his position; that she already has enough of a financial safety net with her assets and what he intends to leave to her in his will. However, as soon as they finished reading the letters and we were beginning to discuss how both letters were very empathetic, they quickly "reverted" to a discussion of the issue itself, rather than continuing to focus on how to use their empathy as a powerful tool to improve their communication. Predictably, within a few moments his anger began to surface, with him raising his voice and making critical comments of how foolish her point of view is and how she does not understand reality of the "proper handling" of financial assets in this kind of situation. Of significance is the fact that Roy was obviously angry as soon as he arrived at this session, as he came a few minutes late and complained of the traffic getting here, saying it took forty minutes when it should have been a twenty-minute drive. His demeanor suggested that he was barely containing his rage at the traffic situation. As our session proceeded, this angry demeanor continued, at one point leading him to angrily confront me when I made an observation supporting something that Courtney had said, namely, that often while talking with her about these issues, he laughs at her. He vehemently denied this, and when I ventured to say that I did observe him laughing, his anger was directed at me: he passive-aggressively yelled, "OK, I get it. I promise I'll never laugh again."

Courtney was trying to take a receptive, emotionally open posture in her reaction to Roy, but at times she became quite tearful as she tried to express how helpless, hurt, and demeaned she feels in this kind of situation, namely, when he takes over in an angry tirade, and then withdraws and is unapproachable.

As the session proceeded, we focused on the fact that the most important underlying issue is the *way* in which they communicate, more so than the actual "content" of the argument. Their exchanges are filled with vindictive and accusatory words, with Roy often launching into profanity, apparently not caring that his words are overwhelming and hurtful to her and then he gives her little room to respond. I even took the step of pointing out that he seems to have a significant anger problem. He reacted with a combination of "going on the offensive" by verbally attacking his wife as the "cause" of his reaction, but he also seemed to imply that he really has been aware of the fact that he has anger issues. Courtney interjected that, in her point of view, he does have a "major" anger problem. I pointed out that her need to interject her opinion right at the moment he was admitting to an anger problem seemed to be her attempt to "seize the moment" and "prove" to me that he is really "the bad guy." However, we saw that she contributes to the problem as well through these kinds of "glancing blows" she makes in the form of sarcastic comments, as well as her mode of withdrawing, including withholding any form of physical affection, even though she continues to fulfill all of her day-to-day responsibilities as mother and wife. Thus, we have a very complicated situation in which we need to deal not only with communication and conflict resolution, but also Roy's anger issue.

At the end of each session, especially sessions which end with active tension in the room, I typically try to find some appropriate "homework" to help clients take steps to address the specific issue causing the tension. In this case, I suggested that they agree to communicate without the use of any hurtful or pejorative comments, taking the time necessary to make sure that each person understands the other person's feelings before trying to respond, allowing for "timeouts" when it appears that an impasse has been reached or tensions escalate, and focusing primarily on talking with each other in a respectful manner. In order to help with this process, I suggested they use a specific technique which has proven to be extremely effective in the kind of situation where communication breaks down due to continuing a discussion while it is not clear if each person understands what the other one is trying to convey. The technique involves the use of a pencil or some other object to be held by a person who is attempting to convey their feelings or thoughts on a particular issue. After finishing the communication, with the other person listening without any comment, the pencil is then given to the listener who now must first briefly summarize what he or she thinks the other person said. The original speaker must agree that the listener accurately reflected back what was said before a response is offered. While the person who now has the pencil is offering his or her response, the other one listens, and then receives the pencil back when the previous speaker is finished and again has to reflect back what he or she thought was expressed, to that person's satisfaction. This mechanism, although initially a bit awkward, supplies a safeguard against proceeding in a discussion before one is sure that he or she understands the other person's position and can reflect it back accurately. When used properly, the power and effectiveness of this technique cannot be overstated.

Rabbi Wecker

Rav Elazar Simcha Wasserman[102] successfully faced many challenges in his life. His father, Rav Elchanan Bunim Wasserman, *Hy"d*, Rosh Yeshiva of the Yeshiva of Baranovich in Lithuania, was on a fundraising visit to the United States when the wicked Nazis invaded his home country. Discarding the pleas of many, he insisted on returning to his family and yeshiva where he succeeded in comforting them as they went to give their lives *al kiddush Hashem* (for the sanctification of Hashem). Rav Elazar Simcha Wasserman survived the Holocaust and went on to found yeshivas in Europe, the United States, and Israel.

He notes that the *Midrash Tanchuma* explains that Noach saw a world that was inhabited, then destroyed, and thereafter repopulated.[103] He suggested that Holocaust survivors study *Parashas Noach* to learn how to adapt to such gut-wrenching and dramatic changes. The Torah records that after the *Mabul* (Flood), Noach planted a vineyard.[104] *Rashi* quotes the Midrash that criticizes Noach for demeaning himself for producing wine and not planting something else.[105] Rav Wasserman questions why Noach would make such an unsavory choice. He answers

---

102   He lived from 1899 to 1992.
103   *Parashas Noach* 5.
104   *Bereishis* 9:20.
105   Ibid.

by suggesting that Noach was depressed after witnessing the destruction wrought by the *Mabul* and sought solace in wine. He then wonders why Noach would be criticized for attempting to comfort himself. Rav Wasserman's resolution may best be described as a clarion call. Noach should have introspected: *Why did Hashem allow me to survive while so many others did not? Certainly it was not to console myself; rather, I was saved in order to rebuild that which was destroyed.*

Although certainly in no measure is it comparable to what Rav Wasserman and other Holocaust survivors experienced, each and every one of us has experienced many "crises" in our lives, some severe and some less severe, but still challenging. Things don't work out the way we expected and hoped. It is incumbent upon us to regroup and rekindle the resolve to continue to work to make this world a better world, and as explained by the *Gra* and others, to work to further *kavod Shamayim* (the honor of Hashem) wherever possible.

SUMMARY

Noach's example should serve as a clarion call. He saw an entire world destroyed, and yet his task was to endeavor to rebuild that lost society in a way that would increase kavod Shamayim in this world. Although we all experience disappointments in life, we must pick ourselves up by our bootstraps and likewise work "l'saken olam b'malchus Shakai—to perfect this world with Hashem's rule."

"I'LL GIVE YOU WHAT YOU WANT, JUST DON'T EXPECT ME TO CHANGE"

Dr. Weissman

Courtney and Roy seemed to be less angry at each other today and more open to communication. He came back from a several-day, work-related trip, and before he left he prepared three envelopes for her to look at, only telling her about them by text message after he left. He requested that she at least look at the first one, although he hoped she would look at all three. She avoided even looking at the envelopes until two days ago because she was involved in her daughter's bridal shower and did not want anything to spoil it. She actually expected the envelope to contain divorce papers. In fact, the first envelope contained a beautiful set of earrings, identical to the expensive earrings he had given her previously but had somehow gotten lost. It also included a love note which was very touching. The second envelope consisted of a much longer letter which was also expressing his love for her and his wish to do what he can to make her happy. The third envelope contained some proposals he had to resolve their conflicts about the estate. This led to a very productive discussion in today's session about different ways in which he is clearly making a huge effort to try and convince her that he loves her and wants to share the assets of the marriage, even though she continues to express feelings of mistrust. At the same time, it was clear that he continues to express himself in ways which are at times demeaning or hurtful to her. Despite this, they both agreed they are actually making progress in their efforts to resolve the issue which brought them to therapy, namely, how to create their wills in such a way as to treat their children—including Katie—equally after both of them die.

However, they also agreed that the deeper problem still involves communication in ways which are hurtful and demeaning. Therefore, we agreed our main focus needs to be on their inability to communicate in a sensitive, thoughtful manner, avoiding any hurtful words. I urged them both to make every effort to continue these discussions about his proposals regarding resolving the issues of their wills and estate, but to keep in mind that the *way* they communicate is much more important than the content of what they are communicating about. A major challenge in this particular situation involves the fact that Roy carries with him an arrogant posture which results in many exchanges in which he is openly demeaning and critical of any thoughts or suggestions his wife might have. He justifies his right to control most decisions by arrogantly saying that he knows more information and that he has skills that she does not possess, and therefore he knows the "right way" to proceed. As a result, Courtney leaves a serious discussion disempowered and feeling helpless in having meaningful input to important decisions. We will have more to say later in the book about the character trait of arrogance, as well as other character traits which are maladaptive from the point of view of developing healthy and fulfilling relationships. We will also see that these character traits are the specific focus of what is involved in incorporating Torah values into one's day-to-day interactions with others and the world.

Rabbi Wecker

Parashas Shelach chronicles the insurrection against Hashem and His agents, Moshe and Aharon, instigated by the *meraglim*, the spies who were sent on a mission to Eretz Yisrael to provide a strategic assessment of the most effective way to enter and conquer the land.[106] They instead returned with a report that Eretz Yisrael was unconquerable, even with the support of Hashem Himself, *chas v'shalom*.[107] (Two of the *meraglim*, Yehoshua and Calev, were *tzaddikim*, and vehemently opposed the report of their ten colleagues.)

Tur Shulchan Aruch quotes the *Baal Halachos Gedolos*: "An optional fast is declared on 7 Elul, the date on which the *meraglim* were killed."[108] *Beis Yosef* (ibid.) questions this statement, noting that the spies were *resha'im* who deserved no commemoration whatsoever. *Beis Yosef* speculates that perhaps the spies attempted to repent but Hashem refused to accept this. We thus acknowledge their failed attempt at *teshuvah*.

Perhaps there is another reason for the institution of this optional fast day. The *Zohar* informs us that the spies were motivated to sin by a desire to retain their positions of power and influence.[109] They were exceedingly arrogant. The fast is meant to drive home to us the fact that *redifas ha'kavod*, literally, running after honor, remains an issue for us to this day. Conceit detracts from a human's quest for spiritual growth.

There is another, even more dramatic, example of how *redifas ha'kavod* can lead to the downfall of even a great man. Yeravam ben Nevat

---

106 *Bamidbar*, chap. 13–14.
107 See *Rashi, Bamidbar* 13:31.
108 Chap. 580.
109 *Bamidbar* 13:3.

was the head of the Sanhedrin during the reign of Shlomo HaMelech. Yeravam rebuked Shlomo for misconduct and became his rival thereafter.[110] The Talmud relates: "Hashem seized his (Yeravam's) garment and said to him: 'Repent, and you and I and Shlomo will stroll together in Gan Eden.' Yeravam replied: 'Who will go first?' Hashem responded: 'Shlomo.' Yeravam retorted: 'If so, I am not interested.'"[111]

Yeravam lost his portion in *Olam Haba*.[112] When discussing the Torah doctrine of free choice, *Rambam* points to Moshe Rabbeinu as the paradigm of the *tzaddik* that one should aspire to emulate, and employs Yeravam as the archetype of the *rasha* whose evil ways one should spurn.[113]

It is truly frightening to contemplate how far a person may fall as a result of an inflated ego.

SUMMARY

Gaavah (arrogance), according to the baalei mussar,[114] is at the root of every sin committed by a human being. An inflated sense of self can cause immeasurable damage to oneself and to others with whom he comes into contact. Anivus (humility), on the other hand, is a foundational step on the way to serving Hashem.

"ONE STEP FORWARD, TWO STEPS BACK"

Dr. Weissman

Often in therapy, we see what appears to be a significant step of progress, but it soon becomes clear that the "progress" is superficial, often involving one partner placating the other, but in a way in which no real change in the dynamics of the relationship takes place. Such was the case in the following session with Courtney and Roy.

It was obvious from the beginning of today's session that there was

---

110   *Sanhedrin* 101b.
111   Ibid., 102a.
112   Ibid., 90a.
113   *Hilchos Teshuvah* 5:2.
114   The various scholars whose work focuses on *mussar* are collectively referred to as the *baalei mussar*.

already tension between them. Courtney opened the session by saying that they did not do their homework, which was to have talked about the proposals that Roy gave her to resolve what has been a crisis—making a decision about how to plan their estate. She went on to say that he made no initiative to talk about proposals, but she reported that she did ask him on two or three occasions. He claims she did so at times that she knew he was extremely busy at work and unable to comply. Most of the session focused on their inability to talk with each other, not only about this issue, but about any substantive issue. We went into detail looking at how both persons undermine good communication, and how the strain on the relationship is such that what could be a very wonderful time in their lives is now fraught with constant underlying tension and bickering. I once again pointed out Roy's anger issues, and by the end of the session they agreed to set the date and time, namely next Tuesday morning, to discuss his proposals and come to some resolution. We discussed how sad and unfortunate it is that the tension between them persists and talked specifically about other ways for them to try and improve communication and nurture the positive aspects of the marital relationship.

Rabbi Wecker

Yiftach was a *shofet* (judge) and leader of the Jewish People.[115] He led the army in a battle against the nation of Ammon. He vowed to Hashem that if his army was victorious in battle and he would return in peace to his house, then "whatever will emerge from the doors of my house and come toward me will be sacrificed as a burnt-offering to Hashem."[116]

The wording of his vow was improper, since his vow included the possibility that a camel, donkey, or other unfit species of animal (or worse) might be offered as a *korban*, and that would be highly disrespectful to Hashem. Sadly, his daughter was the first to greet him upon his return from his successful battle against Ammon. Yiftach was not a *ben Torah*,[117]

---

115 *Sefer Shoftim*, chap. 11.
116 Ibid., 11:31.
117 *Midrash Tanchuma, Parashas Bechukosai* 5.

They Tell Me I Have an Anger Problem 89

and thought that he was obligated to fulfill his vow in the most literal sense and sacrifice her. The story concludes with his daughter either being actually sacrificed or being sequestered and not permitted to marry for the rest of her life.

The Midrash quotes the sage Reish Lakish as teaching that any vow consecrating a human being is halachically null and void.[118] The Midrash records: "Was not Pinchas[119] the *Kohen Gadol* present, and could he not have absolved Yiftach's vow?" Pinchas, however, considered it beneath his station to go to Yiftach. Pinchas reasoned, "Yiftach needs me, and I am both a *Kohen Gadol* and the son of a *Kohen Gadol*. Let him come to me!" Yiftach, for his part, reasoned that he was the leader of the Jewish People, and Pinchas should come to him. The Midrash concludes: "Between the midwife and the expectant mother, the baby was lost!" The unyielding stance of both Yiftach and Pinchas doomed Yiftach's daughter. Both Yiftach and Pinchas were ultimately punished: Yiftach with a debilitating physical ailment and Pinchas with the loss of *nevuah*.

Rav David Luria, author of the *Radal* commentary on the Midrash, quotes the Talmud: "All who are arrogant, if he is wise, he will lose his wisdom; and if he is a *navi*, his *nevuah* will leave him.[120] He suggests that Pinchas acted arrogantly in refusing to visit Yiftach, and he was therefore punished thereafter with a loss of *nevuah*.

It is truly amazing to reflect on the destructive power of *gaavah*. Pinchas, the great defender of the Jewish People, who put his life in danger to stop to a plague that threatened the Jewish People,[121] of whom Hashem said that "he avenged what I, Hashem, should have avenged,"[122] and garnered as a result great *zechusim* (merits); this same Pinchas lost his *nevuah* as a result of acting in a conceited manner. How could anyone be anything but sympathetic to the plight of Yiftach's innocent daughter? If one had the ability to resolve the issue and spare her life

---

118 *Bereishis Rabbah* 60:3, summarized by *Rashi, Shoftim* 11:39.
119 Identified in our tradition as the original Pinchas, the grandson of Aharon, see *Divrei Hayamim 1* 9:20.
120 *Pesachim* 66b.
121 *Bamidbar*, chap. 25.
122 *Rashi* on ibid., 25:11.

or lifestyle (see above), would not only a callous person not intervene?

Yet, *gaavah* causes us to lose perspective, and blinds us to everything but what we perceive to be our indisputable rights. And this is true not only of people in positions of leadership. Each of us, in our circle of family and friends, faces this continuing challenge of putting aside what we (usually falsely) identify as our due. May Hashem help us to see beyond ourselves and truly concern ourselves with the welfare of others.

SUMMARY

Arrogance leads to self-centeredness and myopia, and is the most destructive of all negative middos.

SUCCESS (OR SO IT SEEMS)

We have a concept in therapy referred to as a "flight into health." This takes many forms, but it always involves reaching a sudden agreement or resolution of a conflict, or perhaps a sudden disappearance of a symptom, which appears to indicate a major success or meaningful life change, but which turns out to be only a superficial Band-Aid. Typically, it soon becomes apparent that the change or progress is not as "real" or sustainable as it first appeared. At times the "flight into health" reflects how strongly a patient wants to feel better, or how much a married couple wants to believe that they have resolved an issue. In our work with Courtney and Roy, it was necessary to have a few sessions dedicated to helping them improve their basic communication skills and method of approaching the other person before we could achieve a level of progress that could genuinely qualify as a meaningful improvement in their relationship, or at least a resolution of a major obstacle which had been at the root of ongoing marital tensions. Such was the case with Courtney and Roy.

The previous session appeared to be a major step of progress—Roy's gift of the earrings and his proposals for resolving the issues of their wills. However, this "step of progress" soon appeared to "stall" due to lack of follow-through and a return to hurtful communications. As a result, it was necessary to devote several sessions to the development of communication tools and guidelines which were clearly necessary if any sustained progress in their relationship could be achieved. One session focused on their fear of communicating with each other. Courtney shared her struggle with feelings of anxiety and apprehension when she wants to communicate something to Roy which she fears may result in a negative or angry response. He expressed his frustration when she always raises issues that end up with criticism of him. We went into detail discussing ways to improve this dynamic. At the end of the session I mentioned a specific tool which could be very helpful, namely, whenever one of them has some important issue to bring up, the other person's initial response should be, "You could be right." This would be a way to diffuse the tension at the very beginning of the discussion as well as reducing the tendency to be defensive. They were both very receptive to this suggestion.

After two or three such sessions devoted to communication guidelines and ground rules, Roy began what ended up being our final marital session by saying that he feels they are ready to terminate treatment. They report that they were able to do extremely well in terms of their day-to-day relationship, and that they were able to resolve the issue about their wills and handling of their estate. I gave them the name of an attorney who can help them finalize the documents necessary to handle the estate. Courtney then made reference to having had hurt feelings when Roy had previously asked her to go on a date tonight, but instead he changed the plans so they went out last night. He told her during their date last night that he "might" leave for his golf trip a day early and therefore had to cancel the date he had originally promised, namely tonight. It was certainly a positive step that she expressed her feelings openly, and he was not defensive. He ended up not going on the golf trip so they will be going out tonight as well. We discussed the importance of being able to share feelings openly, while also recognizing the need to give each other "space" if one or the other is not in a position where they feel ready to share feelings. They both agreed that using the communication tools we have worked on has been helpful.

As we will see, the progress they described was real, as they were getting along better without arguments. However, it appeared that the progress was based more on "good behavior" and a willingness to compromise but did not address the deeper issue of Roy's arrogance and anger. In view of their progress, even if superficial, I agreed that we could terminate therapy that night, with the understanding that they would contact me if the need arose. Thus, we terminated marital therapy at that time with "significant progress noted." They both expressed appreciation for the therapeutic work and indicated they would call me in the future if necessary. We concluded therapy with a feeling of accomplishment and optimism. However, even at that time I had my doubts about this truly being a fully successful therapy. I remained concerned about Roy's underlying personality traits which fueled the crisis in the marriage, recognizing that we had not really addressed this in our work. Knowing that he had been resistant to therapy all along, I concluded it was preferable to acknowledge their progress and agree to "terminate" therapy, but I anticipated that what seemed to be a stable situation remained fragile and potentially volatile, and that I was likely to hear from them in the future.

Rabbi Wecker

The *Shulchan Aruch* lauds a *Beis Din* that effects a compromise between two litigants.[123] With regard to the funds of orphans, at its discretion, *Beis Din* may even decide that it is preferable to arrive at a compromise with the creditors to avoid any discord, even if the compromise would deprive the orphans of funds that a strict *din Torah* (judgment according to the letter of Torah law) would award to them.[124]

The Talmud quotes Rabbi Yehoshua ben Korcha:[125] "It is a mitzvah to effect a compromise, as it says: 'You will judge truth and the judgment of peace in your cities.'[126] Which judgment contains elements of peace? That refers to compromise."

Clearly, compromise is an important halachic ideal. There are,

---

123 *Choshen Mishpat* 12:2.
124 Ibid., par. 3.
125 *Sanhedrin* 6b.
126 *Zechariah* 8:16.

however, instances in which compromise is not an ideal—on the contrary, it is detrimental. For example, Torah principles and halachah are simply not negotiable.

Rav Yosef Dov Soloveitchik addressed the issue in a speech in 1975 entitled, "Surrender to the Almighty," in which he stated the following:

> *One must not try to rationalize the chukim (Torah laws whose rationale is unknown to us) from without. One must not judge chukim and mishpatim (Torah laws whose rationales are, at least in part, known to us) in terms of a secular system of values.*
>
> *Secondly, we must not yield to the passing charm of a modern political or ideological slogan because of an inferiority complex. I say not only not to compromise, but even not to yield emotionally, not to feel inferior. It should never occur to one who has accepted ol malchus Shamayim (the yoke of Heaven) that it is important to cooperate even a little bit with a modern trend or secular modern philosophy. In my opinion, Yahadus (Torah Judaism) does not have to apologize to the modern representatives of religious subjectivism. We should have pride in our mesorah.*

The Chafetz Chaim offered the following *mashal* (parable) to illustrate the point. Once upon a time, a king sent his diplomat to another country. At his departure, the king warned him not to accept a bet under any circumstances. The envoy readily agreed. Upon reaching his destination, some officials of the host country pointed to him and laughed. Upon questioning them, he was told that he was obviously a hunchback. He emphatically denied it, and finally the foreign officials bet him ten thousand rubles that he was in fact a hunchback. To refute the charge, all he had to do was to remove his cloak. He then remembered his king's admonition, but rationalized this bet by noting the major sum he would thereby contribute to the royal treasury. Thereupon, he took off his cloak, received the payment, and finished his diplomatic mission.

Upon his return, the first thing the king asked him was whether he had abided by the king's warning not to make any bets. He responded that he had made one bet, and described the circumstances. He said that he was proud of being able to enrich the royal treasury by a handsome sum by simply removing his cloak. The king responded, "You are a fool! I had bet half of my kingdom that no one could make you take off your cloak!"

The Chafetz Chaim concluded by noting that we are all part of Hashem's diplomatic corps. Hashem's orders are clearly spelled out in the Torah and the *Shulchan Aruch*. Some people claim, perhaps even with good intentions, that we must relax the observance of certain *halachos* for the greater good. We must not accede to these requests. Our sacred task is to follow halachah as servants of Hashem and allow Him to orchestrate events to His liking.

One may not take the liberty of deciding what and when Torah principles need to be defended. As with all halachic issues, one must consult with his *rav*.

SUMMARY

Compromise in interpersonal relationships is often a halachic ideal, since all too often we confuse self-interest, real or imagined, with what is right and good. When dealing with Torah principles, however, compromise is counterproductive and never justified. Instead, we are charged to align our lives in their entirety with our sacred mesorah.

"I'VE FINALLY HAD IT— I'M DONE DEALING WITH HIS ANGER"

Dr. Weissman

After a period of almost a full year, it became painfully clear that the "success" we experienced when we terminated therapy previously was fragile. It was based on a compromise that avoided addressing the underlying core issue which was really at the root of the problem. It became clear that real and meaningful change in Roy's basic management of his anger had not occurred, and that he had not really achieved any fundamental change in his view of the roles in the marriage. He still viewed himself as the center of the relationship, as the one who held the power to decide the "correct" path to follow, viewing his wife as secondary. I found myself reflecting on our decision last year that we end therapy at the time that a "compromise" had been reached, instead of suggesting a few follow-up sessions in order to see if their progress would continue. I recall having the strong impression that Roy was resistant to going any further, as he believed that he was the one who made a huge "concession" in order to meet his wife's requests. This "concession" can be seen as an example the kind of "compromise" which does not work because it did not address an essential truth regarding the equal role both husband and wife play in the marriage. At that time, I agreed that we end therapy when a "compromise" was reached. I felt that it would be better to let them "live with the progress" they had made, and to let them discover for themselves whether that level of "progress" was sufficient. Now, a year later, it became clear that the progress was not sufficient. I received a call from Courtney requesting a session for herself.

> Dr. Weissman, Hi, it's Courtney—remember me? You worked with me and my husband about a year ago. This time I'm calling for me. I really have to come to terms with something really important and upsetting that I know I have to resolve. Frankly, I've finally had it—I'm done dealing with his anger.

I was able to schedule an appointment for her several days after her call, and she began that session by saying, "We're still married, but the reason I'm here is because I want to figure out a way to stay married." She went on to explain that she needed help dealing with her husband's severe anger management problem. She gave me information she could not comfortably address during last year's marital therapy. She said that even early in their relationship she was highly distressed by a number of episodes in which he displayed anger at a level far beyond what is acceptable. During these outbursts his behaviors would include yelling improper language and making demeaning comments about her, pounding a table or the wall with his fist, and on some occasions throwing objects. These outbursts occurred most frequently in the context of their relationship, but she also knew of times when he had expressed a similar level of anger in other contexts. For example, she recalled an incident that occurred years ago when their youngest son, Ted, was graduating from high school, and their other son, Cole, came back from college to celebrate the occasion. It turned out that Cole, along with a number of other teenagers there, ended up drinking beer. Roy walked in on them and lost his temper, screaming at Cole in front of the entire gathering, and at one point pushing him so he fell down on the bed. Roy continued his aggressive outburst and eventually had to be restrained by a friend of his who took him outside to allow him time to "cool off."

A more recent incident occurred when her daughter, Katie, was visiting from Washington, D.C. Katie was getting ready to return home and she and Courtney were talking outside in the front yard when Courtney noticed a black snake in the yard. Courtney recognized that it was not dangerous, so she asked Roy to not harm the snake, noting that black snakes are good at catching rats. However, he exploded in anger when she tried to get reassurances from him that he would not kill the snake. She explained that she felt she needed to ask for extra reassurance due to the many times in the past when she has made requests which he intentionally ignored. This outburst was demeaning of her and upsetting to everyone present. She went on to describe a prior incident which occurred at Cole's college graduation. She explained that Roy became openly irritated when she questioned him about some plans he was making that involved getting everyone together, but he would not tell her what the plan was. When she attempted to get him to tell her what the plans were, he exploded in anger, once again yelling inappropriate and demeaning comments. It was this most recent incident that led Courtney to contact me. Since that incident she has found herself withdrawing from him, with the realization that this was not a good solution to the problem.

At this point in the session, I questioned why she has tolerated these anger outbursts for so long. She answered by saying that she always has wanted to save the marriage and keep the family intact, and therefore would try to avoid conflict and wait until his inevitable apology came, sometimes days later. She now finds herself fed up with the situation and feels that she cannot tolerate this any longer. She responded positively when I pointed out that a person with her level of accomplishment, intellectual ability, and emotional maturity should have high enough self-esteem such that she would not tolerate this kind of treatment. While agreeing with this, she also said that she is afraid of his reaction if she were to stand up to him.

As the session concluded, Courtney expressed apprehension about what she should tell him when he asked her about her session with me. I suggested that she not discuss details of tonight's appointment with him, even though he knows she came and he told her that he is "nervous" about it—he knows she is resuming therapy because of the high level of tension in their marriage. Instead, we decided that she simply tell him that she "left the session with a lot to think about," and that "she needs time to process it all." I explained that it would be helpful for him to not know for sure what is on her mind, as this might increase the probability of him more actively reflecting on his own role in the relationship problems. She was comfortable with that plan, and indicated her desire to continue therapy for herself, although we both understood that at some point she may want her husband to join the therapy process.

Rabbi Wecker

The Talmud relates that Rabbi Eliezer (ben Horkanus) served as *shaliach tzibbur* (the person who leads a prayer service) and recited the special *Amidah* of twenty-four blessings that was enacted on special fast days during a severe drought, but his prayers for rain were not answered. Rabbi Akiva then went to the *amud* (lectern where the person leading the service stands) and prayed: "Our Father, Our King, we have no king but You! Our Father, Our King, for Your sake have compassion on us!" Immediately thereafter, the rains fell. The Sages thought ill of Rabbi Eliezer until a *bas kol* (heavenly voice) announced: It is not because Rabbi Akiva is greater than Rabbi Eliezer (that the former was answered in prayer and the latter was not), but because Rabbi Akiva is a forgiving person, whereas Rabbi Eliezer is not a forgiving person.[127]

Rav Yisrael Salanter notes that Hillel and Shammai disagreed about this very issue.[128] Shammai appeared to be quick-tempered while Hillel was tolerant and humble. If Shammai had felt that it was appropriate to be more forgiving, then he would have adopted that approach and not have been so strict with the candidate for conversion.[129] Shammai felt, however, that a strict approach would better uphold the dignity and respect due the Torah. Hillel disagreed with Shammai and felt it more appropriate to display tolerance and humility.

It is important to note that Shammai is quoted as saying, "All should be welcomed with a cheerful disposition."[130] In light of our analysis, we must conclude that Shammai adopted a more severe persona only when dealing with issues related to the dignity and respect due the Torah. Otherwise, Shammai was a tolerant and welcoming person. In light of this explanation, we can understand an important comment on this Mishnah from *Avos*. Rav Chaim of Volozhin,[131] in his *Ruach Chaim* commentary on *Pirkei Avos*, notes that Shammai's cheerful disposition was based upon a sense of humility.[132] Shammai reasoned that he must greet everyone cheerfully since his guest quite possibly had been more diligent in fulfilling his spiritual potential than he.

This area of disagreement between Hillel and Shammai is a halachic issue no less significant than any of the many other areas of disagreement between them.[133] As is often the case, both approaches are valid. The Talmud states with regard to halachic disputes: "These and these are the words of the living G-d."[134] Both sides of a *machlokes* are considered to be correct in essence. The fact that the halachah follows a

---

127 *Taanis* 25b.
128 *Ohr Yisrael*, letter 28.
129 *Shabbos* 31a.
130 *Avos* 1:15.
131 He lived from 1749 to 1821.
132 Ibid.
133 E.g., *Yevamos* 13a.
134 *Eruvin* 13b.

certain view does not invalidate the opposing view; instead, it merely clarifies what the normative practice should be. Indeed, regarding the dispute between Hillel and Shammai (and their respective students, Beis Hillel and Beis Shammai), the *Arizal* is quoted by *Mikdash Melech*[135] as maintaining that in the era of Mashiach, the halachah will switch and follow the view of Beis Shammai. In our pre-Mashiach times we are obliged to follow Hillel's view and be exceedingly humble and forgiving, as noted by *Rambam*.[136]

In another context, *Rambam* writes that Moshe's sin at Mei Merivah[137] involved Moshe's display of anger when he said: "Listen to me, you rebels."[138] The people inferred from Moshe's words that Hashem was angry with them, and that was not the case. Moshe served as Hashem's messenger, and he sinned by giving this false impression. Thus, according to *Rambam*, the one sin that led to Moshe being denied entry to Eretz Yisrael resulted from his exhibition of anger.[139]

Rav Moshe Feinstein remarked that he by nature had a fierce temper. He worked to refine his *middos* (character traits) and successfully effected a major change in his personality by ridding himself of a propensity to anger.

A *maggid* (preacher) once approached the Chafetz Chaim and complained that no matter how much he screamed and carried on, his audiences did not repent. The Chafetz Chaim responded by asking him why he thought that the mitzvah of *tochachah* (offering rebuke) was accomplished by acting in that manner. Do you scream and yell when you put on *tefillin*, the Chafetz Chaim asked?

Rav Yisrael Salanter concludes that Rabbi Eliezer was a *talmid* of Shammai and followed his view, while Rabbi Akiva as a *talmid* of Hillel followed the latter's view. The Talmud concludes that the approach advocated by Hillel was the more effective one in prayer and in producing the desired end to the drought.

---

135 Commentary on the *Zohar*, *Bereishis* 17b.
136 *Hilchos Deos* 2:3.
137 *Bamidbar* 20:7–13.
138 Ibid., 20:10.
139 *Shemonah Perakim*, chap. 4.

Sefer Orach Mesharim points out that anger rarely serves any positive purpose.[140] Anger can often lead to other sins, since an angry person is simply not in control of his actions. *Rambam* notes that with regard to both arrogance and anger, one should not strive for the "golden mean" between the two extremes as with other *middos*, but should instead veer to the opposite pole and seek to eradicate these evil traits.[141]

SUMMARY

Anger is a destructive middah which can easily lead one to commit many sins. Anger rarely serves any positive purpose. There is no "golden mean" with regard to either anger or arrogance. Instead, we should strive to minimize utilizing either of these evil character traits. Great gedolim have by example demonstrated the effectiveness and propriety of an even-tempered approach in life.

"WOULDN'T YOU BE ANGRY IF EVERYONE IN YOUR LIFE ALWAYS MESSED EVERYTHING UP?"

Dr. Weissman

As referenced in the preceding *d'var Torah*, anger and arrogance are linked. At the root of someone's sense of entitlement to express anger without restraint is the personality trait of arrogance. Synonyms for arrogance include conceit, pride, self-importance, and hubris. Clinically, this character trait is reflected in the term "narcissism." At some level, the chronically angry person believes that he should be in control of everything, that things should go the way he thinks they should go. At the deepest level, he feels he runs the world. From the Jewish perspective, this kind of narcissistically driven anger is akin to idol worship—a most grievous sin—as it is as if the individual sees *himself* as G-d, the true Ruler of the world. When others don't comply, he feels entitled to lash out, demand compliance, or inflict some form of "punishment." This may take the form of demeaning comments, giving the other

---

140 Chap. 19.
141 *Hilchos Deos*, chap. 1–2.

person the silent treatment, withdrawal of love, control of all decisions, and in some cases, even physical punishment.

Interestingly, all three of the cases we have been discussing throughout this book capture the essence of this issue, i.e., narcissistically driven anger and efforts to control, criticize, or judge another person. Let's look at an excerpt from each of the cases to see how arrogance or narcissism manifests itself in the dynamics of marital relationships.

Our first therapy case centered around Mrs. Kline gradually developing an "addiction" to her smartphone and iPad, and spending more and more of her time "connecting" with friends and playing games. She was finding herself spending less time with her husband and feeling devoid of romantic love for him. Mr. Kline was always soft-spoken and ostensibly accepting of the fact that his wife was experiencing an internal struggle which only she could sort out. The very fact of his "acceptance" of her dilemma reflects an underlying attitude of superiority and even arrogance, as he frequently expressed his "concern" for his wife's soul and for the fact that she would have to "live with" her decision to neglect her marriage. Additionally, his nonstop efforts to please her through his "acceptance" of her struggle and by taking on as much of the household responsibilities as he could to show her what a good husband he was actually only served to make her feel inferior and undeserving of his love. The result was Mrs. Kline feeling a persistent sense of guilt and inadequacy. Sometimes the approach used by Mr. Kline is referred to as "killing with kindness." Regardless of the "gift wrap" used to camouflage his judgmental, highly critical posture, the end result was to transform the relationship into one with a "good guy" and a "bad guy." A corollary to that dynamic was Mrs. Kline's persistent feeling of not being entitled to express her criticism of his possessiveness and tendency to be "clingy" and make her feel badly any time she was not paying attention to him.

Our second case (George and Jennifer) is a more typical example of the role arrogance plays out in a situation of persistent marital conflict and tension. In that case we saw that George had a complex set of expectations as to how Jennifer should handle her role as mother and wife. He expected a neat and orderly house when he got home from work, with the kids already bathed and ready for dinner and then bedtime, his wife also having showered and looking nice for him. He had his notions of the "right way" to handle everything, and any departure from that would result in open criticism or passive-aggressive withdrawal as a way to punish her. In this case we eventually were able to see how George's underlying insecurities actually "drove him" to hide these feelings by adopting the role of final judge and arbiter as to how she should run the house.

Our third case involved Courtney's eventual refusal to put up with her husband's angry outbursts, which usually included overtly demeaning comments. In this case, Roy's arrogant and narcissistic character traits were deeply rooted and overtly toxic to the relationship, leaving Courtney feeling relegated to the role of a "subordinate," having to comply with his expectations and wishes. More so than in the other cases, Courtney reached a point of "rebellion" against her husband's narcissistic, controlling behaviors. Perhaps the best illustration of this was her eventual ultimatum regarding his aggressive, often dangerous driving habits. She came to a session in a distressed emotional state, reporting that Roy's anger over a minor issue escalated to an intense level of anger as he drove her home from visiting their son in college. He was speeding excessively and they had to use winding, unfamiliar roads to avoid a huge traffic jam, refusing to listen to Courtney's pleas for him to slow down or let her out of the car. Our session focused on the urgency of confronting him about this dangerous acting out. We agreed it required some form of ultimatum, not only for her safety and the safety of other passengers in his car, but for other drivers as well. Also, the ultimatum serves as a way to reestablish her role in the marriage as someone he supposedly loves and cares about — someone whose needs, feelings, and preferences matter.

Ultimately, we have seen in the arrogant person a tendency to blame everyone else for "messing things up" or "not doing things the right way," rather than recognizing that he or she does not really have a "monopoly" on knowing the correct or best way to handle any particular situation.

Rabbi Wecker

Leaders of Klal Yisrael have invariably acted with great humility. Rav Moshe Feinstein addressed the issue of Moshe Rabbeinu's reticence to accept the mission Hashem wished to entrust to him. It took many days of persuasion at the episode of the burning bush, Chazal say, before he could be induced to accept his assignment as the leader of his people. Rav Moshe noted that the Talmud relates that Rabbi Zeira undertook one hundred fasts in prayer to Hashem to spare the life of his *chaver*, Rabbi Elazar.[142] Rabbi Zeira sought to ensure that Rabbi Elazar would be able to continue in his role of communal leadership, and that that burden would not fall to Rabbi Zeira. Rav Moshe posited that we see clearly demonstrated in these situations a tension between one's personal spiritual development and the pressing needs of the community. Moshe Rabbeinu was in effect inviting Hashem to find someone else to take the mantle of leadership and leave him free to pursue his own spiritual quests. Only where no other suitable candidate can be found is one obligated to put aside his own needs for those of the community at large. Once Moshe Rabbeinu was apprised that this was indeed the case, he willingly cast himself into the public arena with complete and heartfelt dedication to his sacred tasks.

Rav Moshe conducted his affairs with modesty and humility, with no thought of personal gain. The Talmud relates in the name of Rabbi Pinchas ben Chama that someone whose family member is seriously ill should ask a *talmid chacham* to pray for the welfare of the infirm relative.[143] Thus, he was often asked to pray for the infirm. He records the following:

> And the only reason I receive these requests to pray for the infirm is due to the fact that the petitioners regard me as a talmid chacham.[144] I am, however, certainly far from being the sage that Rabbi Pinchas ben Chama spoke about, and am indeed far from being a Torah leader of the many generations thereafter.
>
> Even though I do not regard myself as having reached even the threshold of wisdom, since the patient does regard me as such I will follow in the path directed by Rabbi Pinchas ben Chama.

---

142 *Bava Metzia* 85a.
143 *Bava Basra* 116a.
144 *Igros Moshe, Yoreh Deah* 4:51.

> *In the merit of his belief in the words of Chazal, may Hashem accept my tefillos and berachos.*

Rav Dovid Feinstein, *shlita*, commented about his illustrious father, Rav Moshe: "I took my father's *anavah* (humility) for granted. This is what I always saw. He had no *gaavah* (arrogance) whatsoever. If he told someone, 'If you have a *sh'eilah* (halachah question), come and ask me,' this was because he wanted to help the person, to give him *chizuk*."[145]

Rav Yosef Dov Soloveitchik spoke about these issues as well:

> *When imminent annihilation confronts the Jew, Hashem always sends His agent(s) to save His people. Mordechai and Esther assumed this role in Persia, just as Moshe had been mandated to do in Egypt.*
>
> *In Shemos we note that Hashem heard the cries of the suffering Jews and He was ready for the redemption. What delayed it? Moshe was not yet ready for his mission and G-d waited, because He only works through a human agent. It took seven days of persuasion, our sages say, before Moshe, in his overwhelming humility, could be induced to accept the assignment.*

Rav Yisrael Salanter said that one should purge oneself of any self-interest even with regard to mitzvah observance, i.e., he should forego the opportunity to fulfill a mitzvah and allow his fellow to do so in his stead. As an illustration of this principle, Rav Laizer Gordon, the Rav and Rosh Yeshiva of Telshe, asked his *rebbi*, Rav Yisrael Salanter, to be present when the philanthropist Baron David Guenzburg came to visit Telshe. Rav Laizer showed his eminent guests hundreds of *talmidim* studying Torah and began dancing for joy. Rav Yisrael asked Rav Laizer if he would also dance for joy if he saw hundreds of *talmidim*

---

145 Finkelman, Shimon, and Nosson Sherman, *Reb Moshe* (ArtScroll, 1986), p. 430j.

studying Torah in another yeshiva that was not his own.[146] Rav Yisrael probed, "Are you happy because many *talmidim* are studying Torah, or are you happy because they are studying Torah in *your* yeshiva?"

In another example of the efforts of *baalei mussar* to purge themselves of any taint of self-interest, Rav Yaakov Kamenetsky[147] suggested that Rav Nosson Tzvi Finkel,[148] the famed Alter (and founder) of Slabodka Yeshiva, "did not want to exist; he wanted it to be forgotten that such a man ever existed."[149] To further that end, the Alter would feign ignorance when asked what his role was in his yeshiva.

The Kelm approach of not placing *matzeivos* at their gravesites illustrates the lengths they would go to weed out any trace of *gaavah*.[150]

SUMMARY

Gedolei Torah always manifested a heartfelt sense of humility. Some gedolim took it a step further, going to extraordinary lengths to purge themselves of any flaw of self-interest. Although we cannot aspire to their level of shleimus, we must be ever vigilant about the corrosive effect of self-interest on our interpersonal relationships.

---

146 Kamenetsky, Nathan, *Making of a Gadol*, pp. 850–851.
147 He lived from 1891 to 1986.
148 He lived from 1849 to 1927.
149 Ibid., p. 380.
150 Ibid.

CHAPTER FIVE

I Don't Know Why I'm So Depressed

Dr. Weissman

DEPRESSION IS PERHAPS THE MOST FREQUENT presenting issue which compels someone to seek therapy. As we will see, the Torah has a lot to say about this issue, and a great deal to say about how Hashem expects us to experience life with joy and appreciation for our many blessings. First, let's delve into a new case which illustrates some of the factors which contribute to a depressed outlook on life.

John is a sixty-eight-year-old Caucasian male who was referred to me by a psychologist who is presently working with John's wife, Gina. The immediate precipitants for John's decision to get into therapy stem from recent events in the marriage. However, it also appears that there have been long-standing, unaddressed conflicts in this marriage which have damaged the relationship, and have contributed to the patient's experience of depression at times, which in turn triggers other areas of self-doubt. Thus, the patient is coming to therapy to deal with the immediate distress he feels related to the marriage, but is also recognizing another, deeper struggle he has had with self-doubt and a tendency to suppress his feelings.

John began the session by saying that he actually saw the psychologist who recommended me in the 1980s in relation to the divorce he was going through at that time. The situation at that time must have been quite dire, as he ended up getting full custody of both of their daughters. He says: "My ex-wife accused me of being abusive, which was totally nonsense, and the charge was dismissed as soon as authorities began looking into it." He then jumped to the present, saying that his present wife currently sees the same therapist he met with in the 1980s for individual therapy. Just as he was saying this, he began to cry while saying that he is here for two reasons. First, to deal with the immense guilt he feels over the damage he caused to his marriage. He explained his second reason by saying:

> *I never had a chance to talk to a therapist about me. I really should have continued to see a therapist back then, as I had my own internal emotional pain but didn't address it. You see, I have come to realize that I never really felt in charge of any real life decisions. I kind of wandered through life. Now I'm sixty-eight and looking back on my life and wondering who I really am.*

I inquired about what he meant when he referred to the "damage he has done to his marriage." He explained that he violated the marital trust and, in the process, deeply hurt his wife. He went on to explain that he was originally from a very small town in Illinois and has not been there since graduating high school. He enlisted in the Navy, having a twenty-year history working as an engineer and having obtained a master's degree in engineering. He appears to feel satisfied with his military career and his work as an engineer, and he had recently retired. He thought his marriage of twenty-seven years was certainly going well in terms of getting along with his wife and rarely arguing. The problem surfaced when he returned to Illinois for his fiftieth high school reunion, which he went to alone because his wife felt she would not know anyone there and therefore there was no point undergoing the effort and expense of the trip. He connected with many friends and thoroughly enjoyed the time he spent there. One of the friends with whom he formed a connection was an old friend, Carol. He acknowledges that they both seemed to gravitate toward each other, having had a number of conversations and meals together during the three days of the reunion. He continued to communicate with several of his high school friends by social media after the reunion, including Carol, and he made a point of saying that there was "nothing inappropriate, just friends enjoying exchanging ideas." However, he never mentioned any of this to his wife, anticipating that she might not feel comfortable with him continuing contact with Carol and the other friends. However, she recently discovered the text messages and Facebook exchanges he was having with his old friends. John said:

> *It has been all downhill from there. Now my wife is inconsolably angry at me, saying that she feels betrayed. She is even expressing concern that I may really prefer to be with Carol than with her. Of course, there is no basis to her concern. I never had any feelings for Carol other than the compatibility in talking with each other and recalling our warm friendship from our high school days. There have never been any romantic feelings, and I certainly have no desire to be with her instead of my wife.*

Interestingly, while he states she is still very angry with him, he reports that other aspects of their relationship are actually improving. In particular, he notes that physical affection has always been a problem in their marriage; in fact there has been no gestures of affection in over twenty years. Now, they have begun to enjoy some occasional moments of physical affection. He states that they have not really talked about this, and in many ways there is still distance between them. His primary feeling is guilt over having "betrayed" the marriage and hurt his wife.

Additional background information reveals that John and Gina have been married for twenty-seven years. This is his second marriage, and her third marriage. He has two daughters from his first marriage, Joan (who is married) and Kerry, who is unmarried and apparently doing well. Gina has a forty-eight-year-old daughter, Susan. Apparently, everyone in the family gets along with each other. When I inquired as to the quality of his marriage, he responded by saying, "It's kind of good, comfortable, and looking back before all this happened, it wasn't bad, but there were some things that weren't so good. We didn't have a lot of laughter, and there was always a problem showing physical affection." He went on to say that he is more of an introvert, while she is more openly social. This has worked well for them in terms of their circle of friends and their social activities, but has not helped them develop a feeling of closeness in the marriage. It was at this point in the session that he mentioned how it feels to look back over sixty-eight years of living and not feeling he really chose his own path and direction, adding that he is even unsure of "who I am." There was a depressed tone when he was sharing these thoughts, and he cried several times during the session when he touched on some more sensitive feelings.

Rabbi Wecker

In Moshe Rabbeinu's farewell address to the Jewish People, he prophesies:

> *My (Hashem's) anger will burn against avodah zarah on that day, and I will forsake them.*[151] *And I will hide My face from them, and they will become victims, and many evils and agonies will befall them. They will say on that day, "Is it not because Hashem is not in my midst these evils have come upon me?" But I will certainly have hidden My face on that day because of the evil that they have done, for they turned to avodah zarah.*

Seforno notes that Jewry will say that because Hashem has removed His Shechinah from our midst, all these sufferings have occurred. And by so thinking, they will not turn to Him in prayer and *teshuvah*.[152]

---

151 *Devarim* 31:17–18.
152 Ibid., 31:17.

On the next *pasuk*, *Seforno* notes that Jewry will be mistaken because Hashem's Shechinah was exiled with them. Rather, Hashem says that He will hide His face and decline to save them.

According to *Seforno*'s approach, it seems that a time will come when our people will recognize the evilness of their ways, yet fail to repent since they feel that Hashem is no longer with them.

Yet, this idea appears problematic. *Hakaras ha'cheit*, recognizing one's sinfulness, is, according to many *mefarshim*, the first step on the long road to *teshuvah*. According to *Seforno*, Jewry at this point in time will realize that their terrible persecutions were not, *chas v'shalom*, a chance occurrence, but instead bore the imprint of Hashem's guiding hand. This is certainly a laudable achievement, an important milestone of *hakaras ha'cheit*. If so, what happened? Why did it not lead to the completion of repentance? Why was this process short-circuited?

The answer appears to be that Jewry went wrong at one critical point. In their moment of honesty, they grasped that their entire lives had been wasted. Their world outlook had been based on deceptions and lies. Life held no existential meaning for them anymore. They were overcome with a feeling of despair and depression. They claimed that Hashem is no longer with us! The chasm between Hashem and us is too great to bridge. There is no point in continuing the *teshuvah* process, they rationalized, since all is lost. They were overcome with a sense of depression as a result of their perceived inability to rectify their relationship with Hashem. This in turn led them to a feeling of despair. This was their mistake.

The *baalei mussar* write that it is axiomatic that in order to fulfill the mitzvah of *teshuvah* we must believe that 1) we are guilty of sin, without any justification for our misdeeds; 2) that we are capable of successfully completing the *teshuvah* process; and 3) that Hashem, in His abundant kindness, will accept our sincere attempts to repent. A sinner should realize that Hashem Himself will support his efforts when he repents.

SUMMARY

We believe that Hashem has endowed us with the ability to successfully repent for all of our sins.

Depression and despair are manifestations of a lack of faith and trust in Hashem, and can cause spiritual paralysis and worse, Rachmana litzlan.

"NOTHING GIVES ME ANY PLEASURE ANYMORE"

Dr. Weissman

If one looks closely as the way John summarized his reasons for being in therapy, we can see that immediately after describing how his marriage has been devoid of laughter and affection, he launches into a discussion about his reflections of his life. His pervasive feeling is one in which he does not feel he made his own choices, and therefore was never really fulfilled. His perceived lack of accomplishment leaves him feeling as if he virtually wasted his life. Additionally, we see the consistent pattern of suppressing his feelings in order to avoid conflict or the risk of hurting his wife's feelings. Let's rejoin this case and see how John handled the homework, which was specifically crafted so as to help him get in touch with the feelings he has always suppressed, and to "feel" what it might feel like to express those very same feelings.

> *John: Hi, Doc. That letter you asked me to write was even harder than I thought it would be. I appreciate how quickly you returned my call after last week's session. I was really confused and thought you wanted me to write a letter of apology to my wife, until you clarified that the letter was meant to express the feelings I never openly expressed to her, including some of the negative feelings.*
>
> *Dr. Weissman: You know, John, the fact that you were confused about what the letter was intended to convey is really interesting. In our session I explained that this therapeutic letter would give you a chance to feel what it would be like to express the feelings you always avoided expressing, feelings about your needs in the marriage which were not fulfilled. It appears that it is "automatic" for you to shift into "apology mode"—feeling guilty even in many situations in which you did nothing "wrong." I think we are going to come to see that you feel guilty for even*

having feelings of needing or wanting something from someone, even if it's simply wanting some attention or affection. So, let's jump into your letter—do you mind reading it out loud?"

John: Sure, Doc, no problem. Here goes.

"Dear Gina,

My therapist asked me to write this letter to you to help me get in touch with some feelings he thinks would be important for me to express to you. First, I want to begin by saying how much I love you and never want to hurt you. Now I can see that having ongoing communication with my old high school friends after the reunion, and never telling you about it, felt like a betrayal to you. I am deeply sorry for that. Even though it was just friendly communication with no hint of anything beyond that, I can see that I should not have done that, and certainly not behind your back. You don't deserve to be hurt like that. I was surprised at how nice everyone was at the reunion, how friendly they were, how glad to see me. Got lots of hugs and slaps on the back, and all kinds of stories of how much we really liked each other and how much fun we had together. I hate to admit it, but over the years I think I really missed that. Our marriage has been great, and I have always appreciated all you do for me. Sure, on some occasions I found myself wishing we laughed more, and maybe had more physical affection, but I know we came from very different backgrounds, and that kind of stuff doesn't come naturally to you. Compared to all the good stuff, these little wishes aren't so important. I'm just grateful for having you in my life. If I sometimes seem down in the dumps, don't worry or make a big deal out of it. All I ask is that you forgive me for hurting you."

We can see from the therapeutic letter how difficult it is for John to allow himself to actually identify and *feel* the feelings of frustration and emptiness he has experienced through the years. He minimizes his need to feel loved and cared for and downplays his actual level of hurt and rejection. An even closer examination of his letter shows how uncomfortable he is "owning" even the minimal feelings of frustration expressed in the letter. He begins by making sure she knows that I, his therapist, "made" him write this letter, and he then proceeds to apologize (even though I had just clarified in our phone call that it was not meant to be a letter of apology, but rather a letter expressing his hurt, frustration and anger at having to suppress his wish and need for move affection in the marriage). When I pointed out these observations to him, he immediately reacted with an expression of recognition—accompanied by a visible sense of "relief"—as we both clearly saw not only how difficult it is for him to get in touch with or express such feelings, but we also saw that those underlying feelings were really "there," always lurking beneath the surface.

As John and I continued to explore these feelings, we were able to see that he has always struggled with a "hunger" to feel loved and cared for, despite a lifetime of taking on the role of the "always reliable provider and protector," the "strong but quiet one" who seemed self-sufficient and self-contained. Yet, as he voiced in our initial session, he now looks back on his life and sees that his need to please others was so strong that he never really explored what *he* wanted. As a result of this, he finds that he lacks a personal sense of fulfillment. He now recognizes that he has always been vulnerable to feelings of depression and emptiness. We discussed that no one ever really gets away with denying important feelings, such as a longing for affection, without those unmet needs gaining expression through an "indirect channel." Often, and as is the case with John, the indirect channel to express hurt or anger is to sink into a lifestyle and personal demeanor characterized by not enjoying life. It is as if the person is letting others know how much pain "they" have caused him. It is as if one is trying to punish others by hoping they will somehow "get it," that they will see that his sadness is their fault, caused by not showing him enough love and affection.

John's depression is his way of communicating hurt and anger, in heavily disguised form. In the fields of psychology and psychotherapy, we have a very ominous sounding clinical term that captures the essence of this way of handling hurt and anger—"sadism through masochism." This means that we let our own suffering become the mechanism to inflict hurt to another, hoping they will feel guilty, and regretful that they didn't meet our needs or expectations. Often, the roots of this mechanism go back to early childhood years. There is little doubt that being a parent is one of the most challenging, difficult, and yet rewarding roles one can play in life. Still, even the "best parents" cannot always be available for each child's unique needs, and we may not fully notice if a child is feeling deprived of our attention. There are more extreme situations in which parental illness, divorce, death, or even abuse can lay down a pattern within a child of hiding his feelings. Nonetheless, these feelings still seek to gain expression, but usually through other modes of expression, such as various forms of "acting out" to get attention, or such as defiance, misbehavior, refusal to interact, etc. Another way to express these "unacceptable" feelings of anger is often to "simply" become depressed. However, this pattern of expressing hurt and anger at unmet needs through acting out, or developing depressive symptoms, is not the only possible outcome in the infinite complexity of human behavior.

We see in this clinical example how depression can be the result of a person's inability to deal with or express angry feelings. In fact, a wide range of feelings which a person considers to be unacceptable, wrong, embarrassing, or subject to disapproval may be suppressed and lead to his depression. Anger is John's primary "forbidden feeling," and we know that anger is considered to be a negative character trait. Should we allow ourselves to experience anger at all? It is important to note that anger is not alone in terms of "negative feelings," which usually correspond to negative character traits. Any and all of the negative feelings corresponding to negative character traits can result in a wide range of symptoms, relationship problems, addictions, and behavioral or adjustment difficulties. In a moment we will take a look at another type of pattern, one which actually can be seen in our case of George and Jennifer. But first let's hear from Rabbi Wecker with his words of wisdom from the Torah.

Rabbi Wecker

There is a fundamental disagreement among Rishonim as to whether one is ever permitted to utilize negative *middos* (character traits). *Sefer*

Orchos Tzaddikim, in the introduction, states that positive *middos* (e.g., humility and shame) should be employed often, and negative *middos* (e.g., anger and pride) should be utilized only sparingly. Although negative *middos* are to be employed cautiously, they may be used on those rare occasions when necessitated.

On the other hand, *Rambam* opines that even in instances where, for example, one may manifest anger, he may merely *exhibit* an angry disposition but must refrain from internalizing such a negative *middah*.[153]

The main point is that we need to do all we can to avoid anger.

Sefer Orchos Tzaddikim notes that anger leads to arrogance, which is an exceedingly negative *middah*, since an angry person will not be willing to admit his mistake.[154] Thus, anger reinforces his sense of superiority. Anger also causes one to err in judgment and can lead to destructive or self-destructive behavior. The Talmud notes that an angry person will not acknowledge even the presence of Hashem Himself.[155] One is especially prone to anger when he is stressed, whatever the cause may be (real or imagined).

One in the throes of a temper tantrum knows no constraints. His state of anger causes him to lose control, to feel and act irrationally, and to become totally oblivious to the outcome of his words and actions. Perhaps this is the rationale for the comment in *Sefer Chassidim*'s that it is prohibited to gaze at someone who is angry.[156] Commentators explain that to do so would only serve to embarrass him in his degraded state.[157]

The great mystic Rav Chaim Vital[158] writes that his *rebbi*, Rav Yitzchak Luria (the *Arizal*), noted that anger can cause greater spiritual harm than any other sin.[159]

Sefer Shoftim ends with the tragic story of the *pilegesh* (concubine)

---

153   *Hilchos Deos* 2:3.
154   *Shaar Ha'kaas*.
155   *Nedarim* 22a.
156   Par. 1126.
157   Culled from the words of Rav Saadyah Chalunah, Rav Dovid Greenhut, and Rav Dovid Afterut.
158   He lived from 1543 to 1620.
159   *Sefer Shaar Hayehudim*.

of Givah, who was ravished and died soon thereafter.[160] A civil war broke out as a result, and tens of thousands of Jews lost their lives. The Talmud places the moral blame for this tragedy squarely on her husband for instilling in her excessive fear,[161] and concludes that excessive anger can lead to the serious sins of immorality, murder, and *chillul Shabbos*.[162] (Anger is often a response to fear, and these emotions often reinforce each other.[163]) *Maharal* notes that the object of excessive fear loses his equilibrium.[164] The angry person has contaminated himself physically and spiritually, and has in addition often caused a *chillul Hashem*.

In *Koheles* it says: "For in much wisdom there is much anger, for one who increases knowledge, increases pain."[165] *Metzudas David* explains that a wise person will understand his fellow's true evil intentions and will become angry at his perceived hypocrisy and duplicitousness.[166] Rav Chaim Shmuelevitz concludes that wisdom is actually hazardous for an angry person.[167] His wisdom will serve to reinforce his anger, thus creating a perilous downward spiral. The clear message is that a truly wise person will endeavor to avoid the risky pitfall of anger.

SUMMARY

An angry person loses all sense of restraint, and can readily commit many serious sins. Both he and the object of his anger can lose their spiritual equilibrium. Anger is often caused by stress, and wise people are especially prone to fits of anger. The truly wise person will endeavor to avoid the snare of anger at all costs.

---

160 Chap. 19–21.
161 *Gittin* 6b.
162 *Sefer Shoftim*, chap. 19. The husband's temper set in motion a series of events that led to her disastrous end.
163 See *Sefer Orchos Tzaddikim, Shaar Hakaas*: "An angry person cannot be an effective *rebbi*, since his students—fearing an angry response—will be afraid to ask him questions…In addition, an angry person is prone to causing some calamity at home as a result of his imposition of a needless amount of fear in his household."
164 Commentary on *Gittin* 6b.
165 1:18.
166 Ibid.
167 See *maamar* 87.

"I'M THE ONE WHO DOES EVERYTHING AROUND HERE—IF I DIDN'T, NOTHING WOULD GET DONE"

Dr. Weissman

The "martyr" and the "perennial victim." A therapist I know once said, "There's no such thing as victims—only volunteers." We all know the type. People who take on every job or task thrown at them, only to end up feeling overwhelmed, underappreciated, and exploited. For some, the goal seems to be to get others to feel sorry for them. For others, this "martyrdom" serves as an excuse to harbor resentments, to blame others, and eventually to let these feelings surface in the form of an angry outbursts and rejection of loved ones. As mentioned above, we will return to the case of George and Jennifer to illustrate another pattern: that of the "martyr" or "victim."

I went to the waiting room to invite George and Jennifer to come back to my office for our regular weekly session, and found George there alone, without Jennifer.

> *I came by myself today because our regular babysitting arrangement fell through, and since my mother couldn't fill in, Jennifer had to return home after her errands instead of meeting me here. I think we started to have a really good discussion about division of labor in the house, just like you suggested last week, but in just a minute or two I see how Jennifer always ends up controlling communications. She immediately starts to complain about how I don't do enough, and she thinks she has to do everything. Plus, she always has to be the one who "wins," the one who is always "right." It feels like we're on opposite sides on just about everything, and she always has to have the last word. This is why I usually don't even try to talk. Plus, when I come home, she is always on her iPad, sitting on the sofa, watching TV, and at the same time deeply involved in her social networking stuff, Facebook, and everything like that. Meanwhile, most evenings I'm the one who takes care of almost all of the household responsibilities. Actually, I feel*

like I'm the servant in the house. I end up bathing the kids and making supper. When she goes upstairs to put the younger kids to bed, she gets mad at me if the two older ones are making noise or not getting ready for bed. She knows that I can't do two things at once. If the baby needs a diaper, I can't at the same time keep our three-year-old from jumping on the table or screaming about something he wants just at that moment. She doesn't get it—she just continues to criticize and complain. Meanwhile, when I come home from work the house is always a mess, with toys everywhere, dishes in the sink, and all kinds of junk on the kitchen counter. She never really goes through the mail or gets rid of junk. She never puts the real mail where it belongs. When we finally do talk for a few minutes it's always about the children's schedules, upcoming events, and that kind of stuff. We never just chill and talk about us. And even if we did try to talk, we would miss some TV shows that we really like. It's useless; I can't see anything really changing, so I just hunker down and do my own thing, making sure I take care of things around the house, but only when I want to, not on her schedule. She should have plenty of time—she's home all day with the kids. I guess they keep her busy a lot, but I still think that most of the time she just lets the kids do their own thing while she's Facebooking and tweeting on the couch.

I listened attentively as he vented these feelings, knowing that Jennifer has her version of who is the "real martyr." Of course, when he mentioned missing TV shows as one of the reasons they don't have time to talk, I challenged him about priorities, asking him what he thinks is more important, TV or taking time to discuss how to work better together and how to improve their marriage. Nonetheless, he persisted in saying that it is primarily Jennifer who would have a hard time redirecting her attention to a conversation. Although he did not articulate it at this point, it was clear that he wants attention from Jennifer, and is "jealous" of how she gives most of her attention to her friends and social media. He offered a helpful formulation regarding the dynamics of the relationship—that it is more adversarial than cooperative, with her always having to prove how deficient he is and how much she has to do. I was able to help him see that the deeper issue is not about who does more, but rather how they fail to communicate in a way that leaves both persons feeling that the other one hears their feelings, and that they want their spouse to feel loved and appreciated. He agreed that communication issues lie at the core of their problems, and therefore we agreed that in our next session it would be very important for him to be fully open with her about his feelings and about his observations about the dynamics of the relationship—thoughts and feelings that he has never really shared with her.

Our session the following week began with me asking George if he had shared any of last week's session with Jennifer. Not surprisingly given their history of poor communication, he stated that "there was never really a good chance to talk." Sometimes, it pays to be direct and so I bluntly asked both of them if they watched any of their favorite TV shows in the past week. Of course, they instantly "confessed" that they watched all of them. No one needed to further clarify the unspoken "priorities" in their relationship. Having established that they, once again, did not make the time to talk, I asked George to fill Jennifer in on our last session, reminding him that we agreed he had a lot to talk about given the important feelings and formulations which surfaced last week. Almost on cue, even before he began share the content of last week's session or to express his feelings (about how much more he does than her, and how she won't let him talk with her without a fight), she became defensive. In her case, just as George had described, her way of being "defensive" is to immediately go on the "offense." And, just as George said (and as was evident in previous sessions), her way of going on the "offense" was to "out-martyr" him, trying to prove how it is really *she* who has to "do everything."

Actually, it was obvious from the beginning of the session that Jennifer and George were upset with each other even before they arrived. As soon as George was about to respond to my request that he summarize last week's session, Jennifer angrily complained:

> Jennifer: He never told me anything about the session he had with you last week. Even if you ask him to talk with me he

won't do it. I'm also upset because he recently went on a three-day military retreat, but he didn't really tell me anything about it, no details, including not telling me what he'd spent so much money on.

George: Hold on a minute. You're the one who is hiding everything from me. You don't let me know the passcodes to your Facebook and Twitter and other social media sites, and you won't even give me any passcodes to any of your bank accounts. How am I supposed to know who you're talking to, or who you might be spending time with during the day? How am I supposed to know how much money you're spending? You know, we always leave these sessions feeling upset with each other, and I'm tired of it. If we can't talk things through and if we're still upset with each other by the end of today's session, I'm going to go alone to the military ball we are supposed to attend together on Friday night. What's the point of going to something like that together if we can't even talk without fighting?!

I confronted George about not sharing anything from last week's session, even though he had agreed to do so. We discussed how they are so preoccupied with trying to prove how much more they do than the other person, that they end up bringing "filters" into their discussions such that they read more negativity into the other person's words or behavior than is actually there. By the end of the session I pointed out how each of them is saying that they want something from the other, specifically more time and attention, and I did my best to encourage them to follow through with this during the coming week, with each of them promising to do at least two or three things that they know would please the other. They seemed receptive to this suggestion.

In this clinical vignette we see how hurt and anger at perceived unmet needs from the other were not expressed directly—not at least until their *indirect* means of expressing these feelings were interpreted in therapy. In their case, instead of simply asking directly for more time and attention, each of them tried to prove how much more *they* did—ostensibly for the other person—and how little the other one did.

There was an interesting advice column in the newspaper a few years ago. Apparently, the previous day the columnist published a letter which described how a particular married couple credited their twenty-seven years of successful marriage to a carefully constructed division of labor. Each of them knew exactly what their own responsibilities were, and each of them knew exactly what the other person's responsibilities were. No conflicts, no arguments—each of them simply had to perform their respective jobs. Not bad—and certainly a workable solution to potential conflicts. However, the column I read was a response to that letter. The couple writing *this* letter said that they came up with a different solution to the challenges of living together, and they credit their method with the success of their forty-year marriage. They wrote:

> *We discovered early in our marriage that the best way to deal with all the things everyone has to do every day is really very simple. If you see something that needs to be done, do it. We don't worry about who might have left the cup on the coffee table or who spilled the milk or who washed the dishes last night. It doesn't matter. It would never occur to either one of us to pass by the coffee cup without picking it up and washing it, or to pass by spilled milk without cleaning it up, or to ignore the dishes in the sink because it was "our turn" last night so now it's the other guy's turn. It's like constantly giving gifts to the person we love and chose to spend our lives with. It almost feels like a "victory" if you happen to get to take care of something before the other person gets to it. No scorekeeping, no resentment, just recognizing that love is all about giving, not about receiving.*

Rabbi Wecker

Sefer Menoras Hame'or quotes the words of a wise woman to her daughter who was about to be married: "Serve your husband as if he were a king. For, if you will act toward him like his maid, he will act as if he were your servant and honor you like a queen. If, however, you try to dominate him, he will be your master, and you will be in his eyes like a maidservant."[168] Needless to say, this advice is appropriate for a man as well: Treat your wife as a queen, for if you try to dictate to her, the result will be discord and dissension.

Rav Aharon Kotler[169] noted that the *shelamim*, the peace-offering sacrifice, is (according to the Midrash[170]) called so because everyone partakes of its meat: the *Mizbei'ach* (the altar), Hashem (as it were), the *Kohanim*, and the owner who brought the *korban*.[171] He explains that when the *Kohanim* and the owner consume the *korban* for the purpose of fulfilling a mitzvah, then and only then is there truly *shalom* (peace). If, however, they eat to satisfy their desires, then no one is happy and there is only animosity. The same idea applies to husbands and wives. If they interact with each other for the sake of serving Hashem, then they will enjoy a peaceful relationship. If, however, each one places his or her own desires at the head, then, sadly, conflict will prevail.

In essence, both of these sources maintain that a successful marriage is one in which both the husband and wife regard themselves as givers and not takers. Each spouse focuses on what he or she needs to do for the other, and not on what his or her expectation is of the other.

It is incumbent upon each spouse to recognize the essential contributions of the other spouse. This idea is aptly explicated by Rav Shimshon Raphael Hirsch:

> *Initially, the word of Hashem[172] introduces man and woman together into the work of creation as human beings, both of them created equally in Hashem's image and designated as His representatives on earth, their positions and tasks*

---

168   *Ner* 3, *klal* 6, *chelek* 4:2.
169   Founder and Rosh Yeshiva of Beth Medrash Govoha in Lakewood, NJ. He lived from 1891 to 1962.
170   See *Rashi, Vayikra* 3:1.
171   Quoted in *Hasimchah Bimono*, p. 190.
172   *Bereishis* 1:27.

being assigned to both of them together. A subsequent pasuk[173] *clearly makes a point of addressing itself particularly to the relationship between man and his wife in order to impress upon the man the paramount value and significance of his wife for every aspect of his own personality and for the fulfillment of his vocation and his life's purpose. As the "subduer of the earth" and as the winner of the material means enabling him to marry and establish a home, the man could easily come to view himself as the only real and indispensable factor on earth and, under the spell of this illusion, to act toward his wife in an overbearing manner. It seems that precisely for this reason the word of Hashem seeks to make man aware of how helpless and joyless he would be without his wife, even in the midst of paradise (Adam and Chavah lived in Gan Eden at his time), no matter what his own strength and insight, and that only his wife can give him the support he needs to make him whole."*[174]

In a similar vein, the Talmud states: "Any unmarried man lives without *simchah*, *berachah*, and goodness."[175] *Maharal* of Prague explains that an unmarried man lacks a sense of existential completeness.[176] Only with the realization of true existential unity and connectedness that marriage creates can he be truly happy and blessed with goodness. That role can only be filled by one's spouse.

---------- SUMMARY ----------

A successful marriage is one in which both spouses commit to give rather than receive. They recognize that only by together developing an existential bond of wholeness can they become fulfilled as human beings and Jews created in Hashem's image.

---

173 Ibid, 2:18.
174 *Collected Writings*, p. 89.
175 *Yevamos* 62b.
176 *Chiddushei Aggados*.

"NO MATTER HOW HARD I TRY, I NEVER FEEL APPRECIATED"

Dr. Weissman

Up to this point, we have seen several types of behavioral patterns and "defense mechanisms" which contribute to a person experiencing symptoms of depression, and we have seen how depression itself can be a learned response, or even an emotional state which is used to punish another. Let's take a look at still one more of the many ways the person who is depressed is actually involved in a very complex set of "mental maneuvers" which, at some level, serve to create or at least perpetuate the state of depression. To give a real-life example of this particular pattern, we will turn to a new case, Molly.

> *I'm here because I'm almost seventy years old and I'm not comfortable with where I am in life at this point. Julie, my new doctor, was worried I that I might have depression, and she's been a good doctor for my parents for many years, so I started seeing her myself because I trust her. Plus, she's right. I am depressed and I think I've been this way for a long time—who knows, maybe forever. I really feel very overwhelmed. I really thought that by this point in my life there would be some freedom, and some possibility to enjoy life, but instead I find myself trapped with responsibilities which I can hardly handle. I'm always making sure everyone else is taken care of, even if they don't appreciate it. I have problems with my marriage, my grown children from my first marriage, and especially my parents. My husband, Mitch, does what he wants and doesn't usually even ask for my opinion, even though I do everything to try to please him. My Mom is ninety-three and my Dad is ninety-four. I know they are going to die, but for now I have to make sure they're OK. It's really unfair and it really makes me see red when it's obvious that they always favored my sister—"the child who can do no wrong"—and even now, all these years later, they still favor her and take advantage of me. I come to the assisted*

living facility almost every day. She's "too busy." I take them to all their medical appointments, and to the grocery, yet I always get yelled at for not doing something exactly how they want. Especially Dad. If I don't turn my father's wheelchair the way he wants me to, it doesn't matter that I'm spending the whole day taking him to his doctor appointments. He seems to take pleasure in criticizing me, including in front of others. You can see how it makes me cry even as I'm trying to tell you about it. On top of all that, approximately two weeks ago the nineteen-year-old son of a close friend of mine committed suicide, and it's been really hard for all of her friends to know what to do, especially me.

Molly went on to say that she has been married for thirty-four years, with this being her second marriage. She began to describe her husband in positive terms, saying he is a wonderful person who early in their relationship repeatedly said that "G-d sent you to me." She states that he also loved her children and served as a caring, attentive stepfather. However, she went on to say that he has had no job for a few years, and that she thinks the marriage is in serious trouble. There has been no real affection for over twenty years. She went on to say that their relationship is more like that of siblings, but they have terrible fights, usually triggered by very minor irritations, such as him not following through with some household chores he promised to do, his tendency to feel that all tasks are beneath him, and even such minor things as differentiating between trash and items to be recycled. She went on to say that she feels that he sees her as beneath him. She described him as a person who is egocentric and arrogant, and she went on to say that, from her point of view, he is a failure, because he has chronically let her down in terms of being a source of stable financial support. When they first met and married, he did not have a job. Eventually, they started a company together. The company's purpose was to furnish the interior design for Navy ships, but over time the Navy began to contract to much larger companies, so they went out of business. They should have declared bankruptcy, but he refused to do so, and eventually they paid off their debt. She states that the closing of his company was a horrible time for them, but especially hard for her because he continued to be so narcissistic and full of himself that he continued to present himself as if he was the "alpha male." She described a particularly stressful time four years ago when she had breast cancer, resulting in a partial mastectomy as well as both chemo and radiation treatment. Although he spent time with her in the hospital, she recalls one occasion when she was undergoing chemotherapy and asked him if he would get some ice for her, but he refused because the ice machine was all the way down the hallway. At this point she said that "I guess I've given up a lot of things," referring not only to trying to get her husband to be more responsive to her needs, but also in terms of never expecting to really be valued or appreciated by anyone, including her parents.

She then described important aspects of her relationship with her parents. She described her father as a "self-made man, very smart and very independent, but always very demanding." He had a successful career as an attorney. At one point, approximately twenty years ago, Molly reports that she tried to help him with some decisions about his "financial affairs" —how he plans to handle things when the time comes to deal with his estate. He became very angry at her for this, and simply declared that he and Molly's mother have made arrangements such that there will be no fighting or conflict between the siblings. She has a younger sister and brother, and her brother is a successful physician. To her distress, several years ago he asked to talk with both Molly and her sister, and at that time declared that her younger sister would be the executor of his estate. Also, when Molly went to the bank on some unrelated business, the teller casually mentioned that she already had all of Molly's information available, and while looking up some information on the computer the teller said, with a surprise, that Molly's name was not listed as a person who had access to her father's safety deposit box. Only her younger sister was mentioned. Molly asked her father about this and he brushed her off simply saying that it was his decision to make. Molly was devastated by this—she feels that she has always been the one that her mother and father rely on to help them with their physical needs.

Molly went on to say that she has always felt like the "least favored child." She has even found herself feeling that there must be something wrong with her for her to be treated this way. She was able to say that she is very angry with her father, but at the same time loves both of her parents and dreads the thought of them dying. I mentioned that perhaps part of her fear is that once her parents die she will no longer have any relationships which are supportive of her self-concept, namely, "the one who is unappreciated." Although my comment was certainly a confrontation as to how she has integrated the feeling of being unappreciated into her self-concept, she nonetheless became tearful in her response to this observation. Her tearful response to this was her recognition that being in the situation involves a *choice* she makes to be in the caregiver role resulted in a lifting of a burden, or more accurately, taking a mask off, at least for that moment. Even this initial session helped her see that, at some level, she is actively *choosing* to perpetuate the same role she has chosen to play most of her life—the "good one" who keeps doing for others but is always unappreciated. Molly saw that it is she who chooses a repetitive pattern of volunteering to be of help and then resents giving the help as soon as she feels that she is being taken advantage of.

As Rabbi Wecker is about to show us, the Torah has a great deal to say about the issue of doing something for the "reward," or to be appreciated, as opposed to doing something purely for the sake of doing it.

Rabbi Wecker

The last chapter of *Pirkei Avos*[177] opens with the following comment of Rabbi Meir: "One who studies Torah for its own sake will merit many things; and furthermore, the entire world's existence is meaningful for his sake alone."

Is there value to studying Torah "not for its own sake"? The Talmud quotes a *baraisa*: "Rebbe Bena'ah said: If one studies Torah *lishmah* (for

---

177 A collection of *baraisos* (collection of *halachos* from Tannaim which were not included in the Mishnah) from *Kallah* 8.

its own sake), it will be a life-giving potion for him...But if he studies Torah *lo lishmah* (not for its own sake), it becomes a lethal poison for him."[178] In contrast, the Talmud quotes Rabbi Yehudah: "One should always occupy oneself with Torah study and mitzvah observance, even if *lo lishmah*, for this will lead him to *lishmah*."[179]

What is meant by *lishmah* and *lo lishmah*? Rashi claims that *lishmah* suggests that one studies Torah to fulfill Hashem's command to do so, while *lo lishmah* refers to one who studies Torah so that he will become an acknowledged *talmid chacham* and receive honor.[180] Other possibilities of the intent of *lo lishmah* include studying Torah in order to avoid Hashem's punishment, or in order to receive reward for doing so,[181] or studying Torah without a commitment to observe the mitzvos.[182] An additional explanation is offered by Tosafos, who maintain that *lo lishmah* refers to someone who intends to use his Torah knowledge to quarrel with others.[183]

Studying Torah for a personal ulterior motive (e.g., for honor), while not rising to the level of *lishmah*, is considered by Tosafos as falling into the category of *lo lishmah* taught by Rabbi Yehudah: "One should always occupy oneself with Torah study and mitzvah observance, even if *lo lishmah*, for this will lead him to *lishmah*." The other categories of *lo lishmah* are those which Rabbi Bena'ah considered to be "a lethal poison for him." To summarize, studying Torah for its own sake, that is, to understand Torah and halachah, is clearly the ideal. A lower level, which although not ideal may lead to the highest level, is to study Torah for a personal ulterior motive, such as for personal honor. Totally unacceptable motivations to study Torah include a desire to mock the Torah or to use one's Torah knowledge as a weapon to demean or harm another person.

Rav Chaim of Volozhin notes that many mistake the concept of Torah study *lishmah* with *deveikus* (feeling an emotional attachment to

---

178   *Taanis* 7a.
179   *Nazir* 23a.
180   *Taanis* 7a.
181   See *Rambam, Hilchos Teshuvah* 10:5.
182   *Tosafos, Sotah* 22b.
183   *Taanis* 7a and *Berachos* 17a.

Hashem).[184] They therefore mistakenly claim that one unable to internalize this feeling of *deveikus* should not study Torah at all, since such an exercise would be worthless.

What, then, is meant by Torah study *lishmah*? Rav Chaim quotes the Rosh: "One's desire should be (solely) for the sake of Torah, to know and understand it, to increase one's knowledge and inquiry, and not to become impudent or arrogant."[185] If one has not yet conditioned himself to reach this high level of intent, as long as he is not at the lower stage of *lo lishmah*, i.e., he intends to fulfill the mitzvos and does not mean to misuse his Torah knowledge to quarrel with others, he may confidently study Torah. His *lo lishmah* Torah study will hopefully soon blossom into *lishmah* Torah study.

Of course, purity of intent and *yiras Shamayim* (fear of Heaven) are important precursors for Torah study. The Talmud states: "Woe to *talmidei chachamim* who have no *yiras Shamayim*."[186] Rav Chaim opines that ideally one should reflect on *yiras Shamayim* and confess his sins for a short time before engaging in Torah study. His intention should be that through his Torah study, he will cleave to Hashem and to His Torah.[187]

Rav Chaim's *rebbi*, the *Gra*, writes that Torah study cultivates heartfelt sentiments, whether for the good or, *chas v'shalom*, the opposite. Therefore, in order to avoid that possible pitfall, both before and after Torah study, one should endeavor to rid himself of negative *middos*.[188]

On a related note, Rav Eliyahu Eliezer Dessler writes that *emunah* (belief) in Hashem is not gained through discussion of philosophical or theological issues, but instead through an evolutionary process as a result of Torah study. Torah study purges us of biases and negative *middos* that can prevent us from developing the requisite *emunah* in Hashem.[189]

---

184 *Nefesh Hachaim* 4:2.
185 *Nedarim* 62a.
186 *Yoma* 72b.
187 *Nefesh Hachaim*, chap. 6.
188 *Even Shlomo*, chap. 1.
189 *Michtav Me'Eliyahu* 3:177.

The Chazon Ish notes that the Torah ennobles us in two different ways. Firstly, the regimen of halachic observance teaches us discipline and restraint. Secondly, Torah study connects our *neshamos* (souls) with the spiritual realms and thereby perfects us.[190]

SUMMARY

One should strive to study Torah for its own sake (lishmah)—to learn and understand Hashem's Torah. Ulterior motives, such as to gain honor as a Torah scholar, are certainly not ideal, but such Torah study is encouraged with the hope that it will lead to lishmah study. On the other hand, studying Torah without a commitment to keep mitzvos, or to utilize Torah knowledge to be quarrelsome, is unacceptable.

Torah study cultivates heartfelt sentiments, whether positive or negative. It is therefore important to reflect on ridding oneself of negative middos both before and after Torah study. Torah study helps refine our personalities and produces well-adjusted people.

The regimen of halachic observance trains us to exercise discipline and restraint. Torah study guides our middos development and produces empathetic and collegial personalities.

---

190 *Sefer Emunah U'bitachon*, chap. 4.

CHAPTER SIX

Middos: Where Torah and Therapy Come Together

IN THE OPENING PARAGRAPH OF THE introduction to this book, we described Torah as the "blueprint for the universe," and as the "owner's manual giving us instructions as to how we should live our lives." It was given by G-d to the Jews, but with a "catch" attached, namely the requirement that "we must live our lives according to the laws and rules contained in it." The "job" the Jews were chosen to do was—and is—to become "a light unto the nations, a beacon focused on bringing all of humanity to a closer relationship with G-d." Following this blueprint for living not only brings us closer to G-d, but also constitutes our sense of purpose—to dedicate ourselves to *tikkun ha'middos*—to perfecting ourselves, and to *tikkun olam*—to repairing and improving the world.

The major premise of this book is that everything which takes place in the therapy office—a venue in which virtually all of life's challenges and dilemmas present themselves—can only be understood and effectively addressed through the application of "the rules for living," i.e., the Torah. These challenges and dilemmas appear in various forms—relationship difficulties, anxiety, depression, and anger, to name a few. Of course, we see aspects of these very same problems emerge in the lives of our Biblical ancestors. As we have seen in many of the *divrei Torah* offered by Rabbi Wecker, our forebears also struggled—albeit on an elevated spiritual level—with family conflicts, anger management issues, sibling rivalry, personal ambition, even violence, just as they also reflected lives which continue to serve as epitomes of kindness, dedication of purpose, striving for peace both within and outside of the home, faith, and a deep love of and yearning for closeness with G-d.

As each clinical issue was presented and discussed in the context of real-life clinical vignettes directly from the therapist's office, we saw that the eternal truths and tools which must be applied to understand and address all of these challenges are contained in the Torah. As a Torah scholar and educator who has dedicated his life to learning and spreading Torah, Rabbi Wecker has illuminated Torah insights into each of these issues. From my perspective as therapist, I have come to learn that I have actually always based my therapeutic interventions on Torah principles—I just didn't realize that this is what I was doing! The "truths" of the Torah are eternal. A Jewish therapist's job is to find the best way to convey those truths in ways that patients can receive and use to bring about change within themselves, their families, their communities, and beyond.

In this final chapter, we will focus on character development through the lens of the Torah. The previous chapters of this book focused on specific symptoms and relationship dilemmas which present themselves in the therapy office. Those chapters focused on "problems" and how to address them in therapy using insights and interventions which have deep roots in the wisdom of the Torah. Some of the "presenting problems" involved such symptoms as depression, anxiety, excessive anger, and narcissism, and some of the relationship dilemmas included marital problems, parent-child issues, and communication difficulties. Now we will see that character development reflects the essence of how Torah and psychotherapy merge. We will see how Torah principles serve as the literal building blocks for the kind of character development which lends itself to the highest levels of personal growth, psychologically healthy living, and meaningful relationships. In this chapter we will focus on *middos*, the term we use for character development.

Rabbi Wecker

The *Gra* writes that man's purpose in living is to break his negative *middos*, "Otherwise, what is life about?"[191] Rav Menachem Man Shach[192] noted that the *Gra* does not suggest that life's purpose is to study Torah.[193] (And I can only imagine the majestic and exalted level of the *Gra's* Torah learning!) Thus, we see that a life devoted to Torah study that does not include an agenda for character development and growth is in itself insufficient to justify one's existence.

Rav Chaim Vital writes: "Exhibiting negative *middos* is much worse than violation of the 613 mitzvos...Therefore, one must be more concerned about negative *middos* than fulfilling mitzvos; for if he will acquire proper *middos*, he will easily fulfill all the mitzvos."[194]

Rav Yisrael Salanter notes that oftentimes the appropriate *middos* for oneself are the opposite of the suitable *middos* in conducting himself with others.[195] *Avos* states: "One's desire for honor removes him from this world."[196] Yet, earlier we are taught: "Who is considered honored? One who honors other people."[197] While we are encouraged to limit our permitted physical pleasures, we must be willing to exert ourselves so others may enjoy those same pleasures. He further asserts that this dichotomy is especially true with regard to the *middah* of humility. While we must continually internalize a profound sense of modesty, we are mandated to treat others with all due respect.

---

191 *Mishlei* 4:13, *Even Shlomo* 1:2.
192 Rosh Yeshiva of the Ponevezh Yeshiva in Bnei Brak. He lived from 1899 to 2001.
193 See *Hagaon*, by Rav Dov Eliach, vol. 2, p. 727, note 2.
194 *Shaarei Kedushah*, part 1, gate 2.
195 *Ohr Yisrael*, letter 30.
196 4:28.
197 *Avos* 4:1.

The role of *yiras Hashem* in *middos* development is highlighted by Rav Mordechai Gifter.[198] He writes:

> *What can make of man a moral being? What will determine his conduct in a moment of crisis? No humanly designed code of ethical conduct can do so. Fear of Hashem is the governing factor in molding the character of man. The truth of this lesson was taught so poignantly when the Kultur Volk became the beast of the Hitler holocaust...Ethical conduct is void of content if it does not stem from the fear of Hashem. It is this fear of Hashem which is the motivating force of moral and ethical conduct in human affairs. When this motivation is removed, society becomes permeated with the lusts, the temptations, and the forms of vice prevalent today.*[199]

Rav Ahron Soloveitchik[200] notes the importance of Torah study and mitzvah observance in *middos* perfection. He notes:

> *The problem of transmitting ethical imperatives is a universal one engaging the interest of all nations and all faiths. For Jews, however, it is part and parcel of educating our youth in the ways of the Torah: transmitting the Sinai experience to them. We have long ago been taught never to separate the so-called ethical precepts from the totality of Torah...For us, to teach ethics is to teach Torah; and to teach Torah is to transmit to our children the Sinai experience.*[201]

The important role of Torah study and mitzvah observance in advancing our efforts of *tikkun ha'middos* is stressed within the Torah narrative. The Torah narrates the three-day journey of the

---

198 Rosh Yeshiva of the Telshe Yeshiva in Cleveland, Ohio. He lived from 1915 to 2001.
199 Kaminetsky, Dr. Joseph, *Building Jewish Ethical Character* (The Fryer Foundation, 1975), pp. 5–6. See also the gloss of *Ramah* on *Shulchan Aruch, Orach Chaim* 1:1.
200 Rosh Yeshiva of Yeshivas Brisk in Chicago and of Yeshiva University. He lived from 1917 to 2001.
201 *Building Jewish Ethical Character*, pp. 12–13.

Jewish People after witnessing the miracles at Yam Suf. They lacked water, and upon arriving at Marah, they bitterly complained to Moshe about their thirst. The *pasuk* records: "He (Moshe) cried out to Hashem, and Hashem showed him a tree. He (Moshe) threw it into the water, and the water became sweet. There He established for the people a law and a decree, and there He tested it."[202] *Rashi* notes that at Marah the Jewish People were given certain *parshiyos* of the Torah, that is, "a law and a decree" to study. He notes further that the people were tested there by Hashem and failed; instead of requesting assistance from Moshe in a proper manner, they reacted with indecorous chutzpah.

Ksav Sofer suggests that the *pasuk* should be understood as if it were inverted. He notes that the Talmud observes that "were it not for our Torah, no nation in the world could withstand the chutzpah of the Jewish People."[203] Once the Jewish People showed their impudence in demanding water from Moshe, it became clear that Torah study and its positive effect on their *middos* could not wait until they reached Mount Sinai and received the Torah. Hashem, as it were, changed tactics and immediately shared with them parts of the Torah so that through Torah study the cleansing process of *tikkun ha'middos* could commence.

SUMMARY

Perfecting one's character is a critical part of spiritual growth; indeed, Torah observance loses its existential purpose in the absence of tikkun ha'middos. Oftentimes, the middos that are appropriate guides for ourselves are the opposite of the middos we should utilize in our interactions with other people. For example, humility is a character trait that is important to develop, but we should nonetheless endeavor to honor others. Fear of Hashem and a general commitment to studying Torah and fulfilling mitzvos are key in middos refinement.

---

202 *Shemos* 15:25.
203 *Beitzah* 25b.

TIKKUN HA'MIDDOS— PERFECTING OURSELVES

Dr. Weissman

This informative and inspiring *d'var Torah* on *tikkun ha'middos* offers a wide-ranging, comprehensive view of the inseparable link between learning Torah and developing—i.e., perfecting—one's character traits. The insights presented in this *d'var Torah* pertain to the overall importance of character development in fulfilling our purpose in this world. Of course, there are many components to character development, and each of these specific components can be shown to have a corresponding symptom or relationship problem which individuals and families bring to the psychotherapist. (Later, we will discuss the important question of the interplay between the rabbi and the therapist as resources for obtaining help.)

In the previous chapters of this book we have addressed five different "categories" of problems which present in the therapy office: Marital problems, child/parenting issues, family dynamics, anger management, and depression. Now let's take a closer look at some of the specific components which constitute the process of self-growth that we call character development.

Not surprisingly, the Torah is infinitely rich in telling us the kinds of character traits we need to cultivate. At the most fundamental level, we are told to model ourselves after Hashem. What does that mean? It means we need to strive to emulate what we understand to be Hashem's *middos*. This gives us all the "information" we need to embark on a process we can call "thoughtful *middos* development." This is the exact "point" where Torah and therapy converge. If one had to summarize a Torah therapeutic approach, it might be "to engage in a relationship with a person for the purpose of helping that person come to recognize his or her power to choose the kind of character traits he/she wants—or needs—to develop in order to live a more fulfilling life with a sense of purpose." What character traits are we talking about?

One approach to take when describing the desirable character traits to work on is to emulate our ancestors—Avraham, Yitzchak, Yaakov,

Sarah, Rivkah, Rachel, and Leah—whose own character traits serve as a resource for us to identify the character traits we should focus on in our personal and spiritual growth. Avraham's greatest attribute is *chessed*, or kindness. Yitzchak represents *gevurah*, which can mean "strength" and "restraint." Yaakov represents *emes*, or truth. Each of our foremothers also lived lives which were exemplary of other character traits, such as devotion to loving-kindness, personal sacrifice, modesty and humility, and strength of character.

Another source of insight into the kinds of character traits we need to develop is found when Hashem reveals his "Thirteen Attributes of Mercy" directly to Moses:

> Hashem, Hashem, G-d, Compassionate, and Gracious, Slow to anger, and Abundant in kindness and truth, Preserver of kindness for thousands of generations, Forgiver of iniquity, willful sin, and error, and Who cleanses—but does not cleanse completely, recalling the iniquity of parents upon children and grandchildren, to the third and fourth generations.[204]

The effort to emulate all of these attributes is a lifelong process requiring dedication, a commitment to learning, and a longing to transform oneself on a continuous basis into a kinder and more loving person.

Another major source of the kinds of character traits we need to either "emulate" or "purge" can be found in the *Sefer Orchos Tzaddikim*. There one finds a list of character traits, both positive and negative, which includes pride, humility, shame, impudence, love, hatred, mercy, cruelty, joy, worry, regret, anger, willingness, envy, zeal, laziness, generosity, miserliness, remembrance, forgetfulness, silence, falsehood, truth, flattery, slander, repentance, Torah, and fear of Heaven. As we explore some of both the "positive" and the "negative" character traits and behavior mentioned in these sources, we will come to see how some of these character traits are "diametrically opposed" to each other. For example, arrogance and humility are "inversely related," such that one

---

204   *Shemos* 34:6–7.

must suppress or eliminate arrogance in order to achieve humility. Similarly, anger as a character trait does not have a clear "opposite" word in Hebrew, but there are a number of terms and concepts that can be contrasted to anger, such as *yishuv ha'daas*, which means "settled." This inverse relationship between many positive and negative character traits leads to a rather beautiful method of incorporating Torah values into the psychotherapeutic process. Namely, instead of a more conventional "problem-focused" approach to therapy, one which directs attention to eliminating negative or hurtful behaviors and associated feelings, the therapist can be more effective if he can help the person embrace the opportunity to develop and cultivate the positive character traits which are the "antidote" to the negative character traits. This perspective—cultivating in each person the desire to become a person who exemplifies positive character traits—is at the very core of my understanding of the remarkable interface between Torah and psychotherapy.

For our purposes, we will choose several character traits which are particularly central to the kind of personal growth which leads to a fulfilling life, with healthy relationships, a sense of purpose, and relatively free of the kinds of symptoms and emotional distress that lead many people to the therapy office. Devoting oneself to developing even one of these characteristics can—and should—become a lifelong pursuit. Working on *all* of them may seem overwhelmingly daunting. That's how many patients feel when they begin therapy and hopefully come to realize that in order to benefit from therapy they cannot focus on "fixing" another person in order to transform them into someone who is better able to meet their needs and wants. The main "job" of therapy is to help each person see that he or she is responsible for his or her *own* character growth and development. It is good to emphasize this perspective when beginning marital therapy. I always try to make a point of saying:

> *I am privileged to do a lot of marital therapy, but I've come to recognize that "marital therapy" doesn't really exist! No one can do therapy with a "marriage." A marriage is an agreement two people make, and no one can do therapy on an "agreement."*

> *Marital therapy is really "two simultaneous individual psychotherapies," in which I help each person focus first on working on their own issues.*

Of course, I'm referring to adult patients—a husband and wife—in making this point. One must be mindful that our behaviors influence others to a greater or lesser degree. This would be most evident in the responsibility parents have to role-model the healthiest character traits in order to inculcate them into their children. This is the main reason many therapists do not do child therapy; they recognize that any efforts they might make when they are with the child for one hour a week are completely overshadowed, or even undone, if the child returns to a family whose marital issues and/or conflicts around parenting issues are the main cause of the child's problems. Instead, I offer "family therapy" with the understanding that the main work—at first, or maybe the *only* work—will focus on how the husband and wife are succeeding and/or failing to role-model the very behaviors they are concerned about in their child! Notice that I focus on how they are succeeding as well as on their shortcomings. At all times, even when simply "collecting information" about the patient, the therapist needs to be assessing the particular character traits the person is bringing to the situation. As we will see with some specific clinical examples in a moment, the work of therapy is to join in with the patient in helping them discover character traits which are problematic, and to use the therapy process to address those character traits.

The reader needs to be aware that, in most cases, prospective patients who are Jewish must first seek spiritual guidance from their *rav* before "jumping into therapy." Character development can and should be addressed with a competent *rav* using Torah insights directly in helping an individual within the context of spiritual guidance. When appropriate, the *rav* may choose to recommend psychotherapy. Of primary importance is the recognition that *tikkun ha'middos* is a lifetime task and should preferably be undertaken under the guidance of a *rav* (and, if appropriate, a therapist). The following clinical vignettes and *divrei Torah* highlight some important examples of character development in the context of psychotherapy, but they should by no means be understood as a thorough treatment of when and how to employ proper *middos*.

Now let us delve into a discussion of how some central character traits manifest themselves in the therapist's office, and how focusing on these traits can bring about lasting benefit to patients. Of necessity, we will focus on only a few of the most significant character traits. Our richest source to help us choose which character traits are of "most significance" is found in what is known as the Mussar Movement, generally viewed as originating from the monumental works of Rav Yisrael Salanter. In fact, major contributions to this school of thought date to much earlier that that—indeed, back to the Torah itself, which is ultimately the source of all we know about character development. One earlier work which many consider to be the "classic *mussar* book" is the seminal work *Path of the Just (Mesillas Yesharim)*, written by Rabbi Moshe Chaim Luzzatto.[205] There is a large consensus among the *baalei mussar* that four character traits can be seen as the most important and significant: *gaavah* (arrogance), *taavah* (lust), *kinah* (jealousy), and *kaas* (anger). Furthermore, there is widespread consensus that of these four *middos*, all of which constitute character traits that we must strive to eliminate, *gaavah* is the most critical to address, as eliminating *gaavah* leads to the elimination of the other three as well. As we know, ultimately, lust, jealousy, and anger all have their roots in arrogance—it is the arrogant person who feels entitled to "lust" after anything he wants, who feels jealous if anyone has someone or something "better" than what he has, and who feels entitled to vent his anger when his needs aren't met. Additionally, one can contrast each of these four "negative *middos*" with a positive character trait, the kinds of traits one should strive to develop and internalize. What follows is a discussion of each of these four negative *middos*, which we will "pair" with "matching" positive *middos*, presenting both clinical illustrations and a Torah perspective for each one. We will see that each of the major positive *middos*, when cultivated and embraced, serve as the antidote to the negative character traits, with the result of positive change within the

---

[205] Italian *gadol*, also known as the *Ramchal*. He lived from 1707 to 1746.

individual and family. We will offer both the conventional "psychological" label for the character trait as well as the Hebrew term for that same character trait, followed by a brief discussion of that character trait with reference to a Torah concept which surfaces in the therapeutic process.

Gaavah (Arrogance) versus *Anavah* (Humility)

From the Torah perspective, *gaavah* is perhaps the most troublesome and potentially destructive of all character traits. Its "antidote," *anavah*, is perhaps the most important character trait to develop and nurture. We will see how these "competing" character traits surface in the therapy office, and how a therapeutic approach which focuses on the development of the positive character trait (instead of the more traditional "problem-focused" or "symptom-focused" approaches) can be far more effective. First, however, let's get a glimpse into what the Torah has to say about these character traits.

Rabbi Wecker

The Mishnah states: "Rav Levitas of Yavneh said: 'Be especially humble, since man's (ultimate) prospect is worms (that is, the grave).'"[206] Rav Chaim of Volozhin comments that one may not be satisfied with an external show of humility; instead, his sense of humility must be heartfelt.[207] Earlier, he says that a truly humble person will not be content with his present level of humility, but must endeavor to reinforce that attitude.[208] He will realize that his Torah knowledge is a gift to him from Hashem, and thus he has no reason to feel proud. He will flee from any honors, and remain pure-hearted in serving Hashem.

The Talmud discusses the evils of arrogance.[209] A conceited person is considered as if he committed idolatry, since—like the idolator—he refuses to submit to Hashem's will.[210] Hashem, as it were, says to the haughty person: "He and I cannot live together in the world."

---

206 *Avos* 4:4.
207 *Ruach Chaim* on ibid.
208 *Ruach Chaim* on 4:1
209 *Sotah* 5a–b.
210 See Bunim, Irving M., *Ethics from Sinai* (Feldheim, 2002), on *Avos* 4:4.

Sefer Orchos Tzaddikim notes that arrogance leads to *machlokes*, envy, hatred, and lust. The arrogant person feels that he is entitled to his heart's desire, and he knows no restraints.

Rambam writes that due to its destructive nature, arrogance stands as an exception to a standard rule of *middos*.[211] With regard to other *middos* (with the additional exception of anger), the golden mean is operative, i.e., one should aim to utilize these *middos* in moderation. For example, one should be neither a spendthrift nor a miser, but should instead strive to act with restraint between these two extremes. Arrogance, on the other hand, is such a negative *middah* that one should endeavor to eliminate it entirely from one's personality.

In contrast to *gaavah*, it is said that one cannot have "too much" humility. Humility is often confused with a low sense of self-worth. In *Bamidbar* it states: "And Moshe was the humblest person, of all the people in the land."[212] Our tradition teaches that Moshe transcribed each and every *pasuk* (passage) that was dictated to him by Hashem. How could Moshe have remained humble under those conditions? He knew that the Torah would record his humility for posterity! Rav Mordechai Gifter answered that Moshe was continually in the presence of Hashem Himself. Any quality he, Moshe, might have possessed over and beyond other people paled into insignificance in comparison to his stature vis-à-vis Hashem Himself. Thus, he felt no sense of arrogance.

A different answer is offered by Rav Henoch Leibowitz. Moshe certainly knew that he was an immeasurably greater Torah authority than anyone else. This was, after all, undeniable. He reasoned, however, that his greatness was the result of the fact that he had been given opportunities that had not been granted to others. His close relationship with Hashem, which included—but was certainly not limited to—being tutored for forty days and nights by Hashem Himself on Mount Sinai, was unique. He thought that if others been offered a similar opportunity and privilege, they would have become as great as he, and maybe even greater.

True humility, then, involves an honest appraisal of one's strengths

---

211 *Hilchos Deos*, chap. 1–2.
212 12:3.

without taking any credit for one's achievements, since both one's aptitude and life experiences were prearranged by Hashem.

Unredeemed *gaavah* is, in the words of the *baalei mussar*, one of the four most destructive *middos*. The other three negative *middos* are lust, jealousy, and anger.[213] My *rebbi*, Rav Zechariah Mines,[214] noted that the other three negative *middos* derive from *gaavah*.[215] Without a misplaced sense of self, man would not have the audacity to sin.

SUMMARY

Arrogance is an abomination to Hashem. The arrogant person's sin is compared to idolatry. Hashem, as it were, says to the haughty person: "He and I cannot live together in the world."

A haughty person feels entitled to hanker after anything that he chooses. He knows no restraints. His attitude can lead to machlokes, envy, hatred, and lust.

Humility is often mistaken for naivete. A truly humble person has a clear perception of his stature, but assumes no credit for whatever accomplishments he may have. Instead, he internalizes the idea that Hashem has offered him opportunities for advancement that may have been denied others. Another person in his situation would have achieved as much as he did, if not more. The humble person also recognizes that he is obligated to use his talents to better himself and support others. Rav Henoch Leibowitz said that in the Slabodka Yeshiva, a popular saying was, "There is no such thing as privilege without responsibility."

Dr. Weissman

As we have seen from some of the cases presented in previous chapters, arrogance, at varying levels of severity, is a surprisingly "common thread" linking what otherwise might seem to be very different personalities and problems. We use the word "narcissism" as a virtual synonym for arrogance. An arrogant person is self-absorbed, feeling a sense of entitlement to power or dominance in a relationship. Sometimes the "power position" may be

---

213 See *Mesillas Yesharim*, chap. 11.
214 Rosh Yeshiva of Yeshivas Chayei Dovid in Queens, New York. He lived from 1928 to 2011.
215 This is based upon the Vilna Gaon's comments, summarized in *Even Sheleimah* 2:1–2.

obvious. For example, in many relationships it is clear that one partner always feels like he or she is being measured by the other. Conversely, the one "holding the yardstick" feels justified, as that person sees only his or her way as the "right" way and that without "making sure it's done right" he or she feels as if others are failing to take responsibility. This is actually a form of narcissism, a feeling of grandiosity accompanied by a lack of empathy for others, a need for appreciation and admiration. Others become one's agents to bring about what the narcissist wants. Road rage is a reaction we see in persons who struggle with *gaavah*, with a sense that they own the road, that everyone should just get out of their way.

In the cases presented earlier, each of the men exhibited arrogance and narcissism. Perhaps these traits are most clearly evident in the case of Roy and Courtney:

> *It doesn't take much to set him off. Even a very small frustration can trigger an intense reaction, like when he was speeding down a narrow, winding road in the mountains. It was downright dangerous, and it started simply because we left to return home about thirty minutes later than he initially wanted. When we left for the drive home, as if to punish us, he decided to depart from our normal route and take what he called a "shortcut," down a road that even a mountain goat couldn't handle. When I asked him to slow down, even begged him, he simply ignored me and continued to drive like a maniac, as if he didn't even hear my distress. He only cares about what he wants, and he always thinks he's right. It makes me feel that I don't count at all.*

Another case which illustrates the emotional damage caused by *gaavah* is that of George and Jennifer.

> *I just don't get why it's so impossible for Jennifer to meet my expectations as to how she should handle being a mother and wife. I expect a neat and orderly house when I get home from work, with the kids already bathed and ready for dinner, and then bedtime. It also shouldn't be so hard for her to be showered.*

> *Even with the kids, she doesn't know how to keep them in line. She lets them run over the house and do anything they want while she's busy looking at her phone or iPad. If she would only listen to me and do things the way they should be done, she might be able to give me more attention, instead of all of her attention going to her attempt to somehow manage the kids. I know how she should handle things, but she just won't listen.*

A slightly deeper look at George's expectations shows not only his arrogance, but also his underlying insecurities. What he is *really* upset about is not getting enough attention. He feels unloved and becomes desperate in his effort to try to get his wife to change. His reaction when she fails to meet his expectations is like a child throwing a temper tantrum. After venting his anger and frustration verbally (i.e., yelling), he then uses passive-aggressive withdrawal as a way to punish her.

A brief review of some of the main therapeutic interventions in these cases illustrates that my specific interventions were all designed to help each individual first focus on his or her own "contribution to the problem." It is necessary to help the person "own" that his perceptions, reactions, and actions also contribute to the problem, and that these collectively reflect a character trait that doesn't serve him well. It then becomes possible to help him see how this character trait impacts, and sometimes damages, everyone in his life. It is only when the patient recognizes that an aspect of his own character is part of the source of his own distress and the distress inflicted onto his family, coworkers, and others, that we can begin to help the patient develop the motivation to develop the "opposite" character trait. Therapeutic interventions highlight the instant reward one feels when being kind instead of critical, interested in the feelings and needs of the other instead of seeing other persons in their life as agents to get what he or she wants. One approach to helping my patient become even slightly interested in working on himself in order to reduce or eliminate *gaavah*, and instead to foster humility, is to facilitate opportunities—usually through homework—to give him a chance to actually experience what it is like to do the opposite of what his normal response would be. Instead of being critical, he should be complementary of the other person's effort or motivation.

Instead of saying something demeaning, he will say something affirmative. One easy-to-remember idea is the fact that in Hebrew the word for "love" is *"ahavah,"* which literally means "to give." If one wants to receive love one must first become a more giving person. Most importantly, each of us actually has the power to *choose* to change how we experience ourselves and how we interact with others by cultivating positive character traits.

Taavah (Lust) versus *Gevurah* (Strength)

Dr. Weissman

Lust is not a word that is used often in the context of the therapy process, although we all know that it refers to an intense or passionate desire for someone or something. It can serve as a powerful driving force behind all decisions we make and actions we take. In psychotherapy jargon we use such terms as "problems with impulse control," or "low frustration tolerance" to explain why an individual might go to extreme measures to satisfy a desire. Perhaps the "clinical" term which most closely correlates with lust is "libido," but it might be too restrictive. One can lust for just about anything—money, fame, luxuries, drugs, etc. In my experience, what is most often seen in the therapist's office as lust presents as an intense desire to "possess" someone or something. One becomes preoccupied with "that person" or "that thing," and a high level of anxiety is felt when one can't have that person or thing, or even worse, if someone else "possesses" that person or thing. The character trait which opposes this is restraint, or in Hebrew, *gevurah*, generally translated as "strength." In this context, *gevurah* refers to the kind of strength which is required to exercise self-discipline, the ability to tolerate frustration, and to control one's impulses. Let's begin with a Torah perspective on this *middah* of *taavah*.

Rabbi Wecker

In *Bamidbar*, we learn that the Jewish People felt a lusting for food other than the *mann* (manna) which had been the mainstay of their diet.[216]

---

216 *Bamidbar* 11:4–9.

When confronted with the demand that he satisfy their lust, Moshe appeared to lose his self-composure. Instead of defending the people before Hashem as he had done after the sin of the Golden Calf,[217] Moshe complained bitterly about the overwhelming burden of leading the Jews, bemoaning the fact that he was expected to act as their "nursing parent."[218]

Why was Moshe's reaction to the people lusting for food so radically different than his reaction to the sin of the Golden Calf? Rav Yosef Dov Soloveitchik explained that the sin of lusting was in a sense more severe than the sin of the Golden Calf. The latter sin involved only exterior pagan practices, whereas the sin of lusting exemplified a pagan way of life, one characterized by boundless lust and desire. Such a lifestyle is incompatible with our Torah which is characterized by moderating one's desires. Unbridled lust is the polar opposite of the restrained, redemptive lifestyle mandated by our sacred traditions.

Moshe bemoaned the fact that he would now have to redouble his efforts to wean the people from their enslavement to their desires, a task that would consume virtually every waking moment of his day.

Ramban notes that it is possible for a person to act in a repulsive and disgusting manner, and yet not violate any specific halachic ruling.[219] One may, for example, scrupulously abide by the laws of kashrus and yet be guilty of disgusting gluttony. He categorizes such an individual as a *"naval b'reshus haTorah,"* a base person acting within the technical guidelines of the Torah. To forestall such behavior, the Torah exhorts us in a general sense, *"Kedoshim tehiyu*—You will be holy." The import of this mitzvah is, according to *Sifrei*, "Sanctify yourself with what is permitted you (by partaking of even acceptable items only in moderation)."[220] Not only must we avoid forbidden items, but we are also mandated to enjoy even permitted pleasures with restraint.

With even a cursory perusal of Torah and *Nevi'im* (Prophets), one notices the continued emphasis on the evils of *avodah zarah* (idolatry).

---

217   *Shemos* 32:11–14.
218   *Bamidbar* 11:10–15.
219   *Vayikra* 19:2.
220   Ibid., 104:7.

The concept of idolatry seems foreign to us. The Talmud records: "Rav Yehudah quoted Rav: 'The Jewish People were well aware of the fact that there was no substance to the belief in idolatry, and the only reason they turned to idol worship was so they could with a clear conscience permit public immorality.'"[221] As my *rebbi* Rav Michel Barenbaum[222] noted, people will often fabricate a "religion" to justify their addiction to sin.

Megillas Esther describes in great detail the society ruled by King Achashveirosh. A sense of permissiveness and hedonism was pervasive. The people worshipped beauty and their desire for it knew no bounds. Unredeemed beauty can lead to great evil. As Rav Yisrael Salanter writes: "A person's imagination (of beauty) knows no bounds, and as a result his reasoning is nonfunctional."[223]

Rav Soloveitchik noted that there was a Gestapo officer who resided in Vilna during the Nazi occupation. He was an accomplished musician. He was ambidextrous, and played Beethoven's *Moonlight Sonata* with his right hand, while his left hand was busy shooting Jewish babies. Somehow, his culture did not prevent him from being a mass murderer.

Only the debauched environment in Shushan could produce the conditions for a royal order mandating the destruction of Jewry, *Rachmana litzlan*.[224] The lusting person has somehow disabled his spiritual equilibrium, his sense of control that would otherwise warn him to avoid dangerous pitfalls. Unbridled lust is evidentially capable of turning a human being into a dangerous beast.

--- SUMMARY ---

A Torah lifestyle is one that demands moderation, even in areas of permitted pleasure. Self-indulgence and hedonism run counter to both the letter and the spirit of halachah.

---

221 *Sanhedrin* 63b.
222 *Mashgiach* at Mesivta Tiferes Yerushalayim. He lived from 1906 to 2003.
223 Letter 1.
224 *Esther* 3:8–15.

Dr. Weissman

In the first chapter of this book, we discussed a case of a woman who was developing addictive behavior with regard to spending hours every day—and evening—connecting with her friends on social media, surfing the internet, and playing video games on her cell phone and iPad. Her involvement in these activities was sufficiently intense and enjoyable that she continued to find reasons to reject and even deprecate her husband's significant steps to respond to her expressed needs. Her level of internal distress was extremely high as she struggled to deal with the conflict between her intense involvement in this kind of activity versus her deeply held values regarding her obligation to devote herself to her marriage. Ultimately, her values prevailed and she was able to "wean herself off" this involvement with social media and begin giving more of herself to her husband and family. She exercised *gevurah*, and not surprisingly, she was only able to do this by an intensification of her commitment to living her life according to her faith. Essentially, she was able to "humble herself in the eyes of G-d," recognizing that her desires were insignificant when compared to her sense of responsibility to honor—through her actions—the commitment she made years earlier to marriage and all the sanctity entailed in that uniquely human and spiritual relationship. She was able to take a major step in the direction of humility, placing her own (selfish) needs below the much higher need to live a life in which she honors her commitment to higher values.

Kinah (Jealousy) versus *Sippuk* (Satisfaction)

Rabbi Wecker

Korach, Moshe's first cousin, instigated a rebellion against Moshe[225] and as a consequence died miraculously and was denied a portion in *Olam Haba*.[226] In *Mesillas Yesharim* it states: "What caused Korach, along with his entire congregation, to be destroyed if not the desire for

---

225 See *Bamidbar* 16.
226 See *Sanhedrin* 109b.

honor? The Torah explicitly states: 'Do you also desire the *kehunah*?'[227] And Chazal claim that Korach initiated the revolt against Moshe when he, Korach, saw Elitzafan ben Uziel appointed prince,[228] when Korach desired to be appointed prince in his stead."[229] Rashi states explicitly that Korach was obsessed by a sense of jealousy.[230]

On the one hand, Korach was a great person. It states in *Bamidbar Rabbah* that Korach was a great Torah scholar, one of the bearers of the *Aron* (the Ark of the *Mishkan*).[231] On the other hand, Talmud Yerushalmi notes that Korach said: "The Torah was not from Hashem, Moshe is not a true *navi*, and Aharon is not a *Kohen Gadol*."[232] The Talmud observes: Korach set his sight on something not fitting for him (i.e., the *kehunah*). As a result, what he sought was not given to him, and what he already possessed was taken from him.[233]

The Mishnah describes the mutiny of Korach and his followers as being the prototype of "a dispute not for the sake of Heaven (Hashem)."[234] *Maharal* explains that there was absolutely no aspect of sincere motivation on the part of Korach in his rebellious acts. He was completely driven by jealousy and a quest for honor.[235]

Rashi[236] quotes the Midrash:[237] But Korach, who was an astute person, what led him to this foolhardy scheme? His eye led him to miscalculate.[238] He saw that a great chain of progeny would descend from him. First, he saw Shmuel HaNavi would descend from him, and he thought: "Because of him I will avoid punishment." Then he saw twenty-four *mishmaros* (families of *Levi'im* who would officiate in the Beis Hamikdash on a rotation).

---

227   *Bamidbar* 16:10.
228   *Bamidbar Rabbah* 18:2.
229   Chap. 11.
230   *Bamidbar* 16:3.
231   Ibid., 3.
232   *Sanhedrin* 10:1.
233   *Sotah* 9b.
234   *Avos* 5:17.
235   Ibid.
236   *Bamidbar* 16:7.
237   *Bamidbar Rabbah*, ibid.
238   *Maharzu*, ibid; his prophetic vision.

Earlier, Moshe had informed Korach that all of the fraudulent candidates for *Kohen* would perish. Korach thought: "Is it possible that these great descendants will issue from me and I will not demand my rights?" All of his family had actively supported Korach in his clash with Moshe. He figured that if his entire family was killed, then the prophecy concerning his great descendants would not come to pass. Thus, he and his family could not die, and that is why he fought to gain the status of *Kohen*.

Korach thought he would emerge victorious in this battle with Moshe, but he did not "see"[239] correctly, for his children would repent for their role in the rebellion, while Moshe saw that Korach would die.

Sefer Orchos Tzaddikim[240] quotes Rebbe Akiva as saying that *teshuvah* is one of seven items whose existence preceded the creation of the universe.[241] The author continues:

> *If this were not so, then the world could not stand for even one generation, for "there is no man on earth who is such a tzaddik that did good and never sinned."*[242] *And if a generation sinned, they would deserve to be destroyed…But (instead) Hashem created teshuvah before He created the universe, and He waits (patiently) from generation to generation (for the sinners to repent).*

How could Korach completely ignore the possibility that his sons would repent? Isn't *teshuvah* a viable option for every sinner? How could a wise person rule out something as basic as the prospect that a sinner would repent?

The answer is that Korach, wise man that he was, was so completely blinded by his negative *middos* of jealousy and seeking honor that he failed to consider the obvious possibility that his sons would repent. Had he done so, his elaborate rationalization for engaging in what can only be termed a suicide mission would have completely unraveled.

---

239 See ibid.
240 Gate 26, *Teshuvah*.
241 *Pesachim* 54a.
242 *Koheles* 7:20.

The Mishnah quoted above contrasts Korach's incentive in confronting Moshe with the halachic disputes between Hillel and Shammai, which are the model of "a dispute for the sake of Heaven (Hashem)."[243] Rav Yeruchom Levovitz, mashgiach of the Mir Yeshiva, suggests that the Mishnah sees an affinity between the respective arguments of Hillel and Shammai on the one hand, and Korach and his co-conspirators on the other.[244] Rav Yeruchom claims that initially Korach was motivated by sincere intentions, just as were Hillel and Shammai. Korach wished to become a *Kohen* so that he could serve Hashem more fully and grow spiritually. Soon, however, his intentions degenerated into coarse jealousy and honor-seeking.

It is truly amazing to introspect on the nature of human frailty. A human being can rapidly fall from the heights of sincere desire to serve Hashem to the lowest depths of self-centeredness, self-aggrandizement, and petty jealousy. It is only after making a concerted effort to rein in one's propensity to act out negative *middos* that we may sincerely and wholeheartedly attempt to accomplish our G-d-given task of perfecting ourselves and the world through *avodas Hashem*.

SUMMARY

Jealousy is one of the most destructive middos. It can blind even a wise person to the simplest, most self-evident truths. Jealousy can completely rob a person—even a great and heretofore sincere person—of any integrity.

Dr. Weissman

Another case we reviewed earlier in the book captures the extent to which an individual can be so caught up in feelings of jealousy that it can "take hold," of the person, virtually imprisoning him or her in a painful position of being caught between longing and anger. Jealousy is potentially disastrous to one's marriage, friendships, and self-concept.

At the beginning of chapter 5, which dealt with depression, we discussed the case of a sixty-eight-year-old man, John, who was married for twenty-seven years to Gina, but whose marriage was threatened

---

243   *Avos* 5:17.
244   Commentary on *Bamidbar* 16:1.

following his attendance at his fiftieth high school reunion. He reconnected with friends he had not seen in all those years, including several women he had dated in high school. He was pleasantly surprised when he realized how pleased almost everyone was to see him, indicating that he was actually much more popular and well-liked than he imagined, and he especially "connected" with several of his closest friends from those days. His correspondence with these friends, including a female friend, continued after the reunion. John did not discuss this with Gina, who became highly distressed when she eventually learned that they were still texting and emailing each other. Gina was overcome with persistent feelings of jealousy and anger at John for not telling her about these communications. Gina eventually joined us in therapy, thereby allowing for a direct focus on the dynamics of the marriage, which was marked by her inability to trust him again. While strongly maintaining that there was nothing inappropriate in his correspondence with these friends, Gina's suspicions and jealousy continued to dominate all interactions between them. She continued to question and doubt him, and as a result, communication between them deteriorated, and the distance between them increased.

What ended up being my last session with this couple was one in which we directly addressed the issue of jealousy. In that session, they began by reporting that they have been doing somewhat better with each other on a day-to-day basis, specifically in terms of trying to communicate more, and they have experienced fewer episodes of tension or conflict. However, it was clear that their conversations have remained neutral and superficial, with an avoidance of any discussion regarding Gina's ongoing mistrust of him. The previous week I had given them homework—to write role-reversal letters in which they each write a letter as if they were the other person, so the letter had to reflect their spouse's view of the marriage. At this point in today's session they took turns reading the role-reversal letters they had each written, and both of these letters showed a great deal of insight as to the feelings and concerns of the other person. Gina remained preoccupied with what she considers to be his inappropriate communications with his male and female high school friends, and stated that it is particularly distressing that he chose to keep these communications from her. She openly admitted that she simply cannot get beyond the point of being stuck in her jealousy and mistrust. She continues to ask him why he kept it secret, and he repeatedly responds by admitting it was wrong and he then again apologizes, which for her is never a satisfactory answer. In view of her ongoing unhappiness at his inability to give her an acceptable answer, one that would help her move on, they agreed to my suggestion that each them take the time to give some serious thought as to what in their opinion the other person could say to satisfy their concerns. In particular, I asked John's wife to give thought as to what he could possibly say that would be satisfactory to her. They both were receptive to this suggestion, and we proceeded to schedule John's next individual session later in the week, at his regular time on Friday, and another conjoint session for the following Tuesday, which suited her schedule.

I received a text message from John the day before our Friday individual session informing me that he had to cancel the next day's appointment due to the fact that they were in the middle of a kitchen renovation. Then, on Sunday evening, I received a second text message from John, in which he said he wanted to cancel all future sessions, simply saying that our last two sessions "were not what I expected nor what I need in the way of help." The message arrived Sunday evening, so I decided to wait before attempting to contact him. I chose to call him the following morning, but had to leave a message simply requesting that he call me back so we could have a moment to explore his decision. He called back a couple of hours later.

We ended up spending over forty-five minutes on the phone in a very enlightening and productive discussion of the actual underlying reasons for choosing to bolt from therapy. At first, he mentioned that in one session I looked tired (in fact, I'd had outpatient surgery the previous day), and that in the other session he wasn't sure I remembered all of the medications he was taking. It didn't take long for him to see that these "issues" were actually excuses for aborting therapy, with the "real" reason being his wife's intense discomfort at my having challenged her to give thought as to what, if anything, John could do to address her concerns. Obviously, she almost instantly knew that there was nothing he could say or do to "erase" her jealousy or anger, apart from the one thing he could *really* do, which was to be a loving husband. Of equal importance during this phone call was the insight that he knows *exactly* why he didn't talk to Gina about his communications with his "reunion friends." He didn't tell her for the same reason he typically avoids any substantive conversation with her—his fear of her reaction. It was easy to recall numerous times when he suppressed his feelings and did not talk with her about anything that might potentially upset her. The most significant example of this is the fact that he *never* spoke with his wife about her almost complete lack of interest in any physical affection, a problem which has pervaded their marriage. So, just as much as Gina did not want to have to "own" that jealousy and mistrust are *her* issues to work through, John has wanted to avoid the anxiety-producing situation of having to actually express his feelings to his wife, especially those which are actually *most* in need of discussing, namely, areas of conflict in the marriage.

John ended the call expressing positive feelings about this conversation and agreeing to give "serious thought" to the issues we discussed. He implied the possibility that he might contact me to resume sessions with the recognition that he *does* have genuine difficulties expressing his feelings. He expressed his recognition that for his own personal growth, he needs to overcome this problem. I also helped him see that his wife would at some point have to come to the realization that her jealousy is toxic and rooted in her own deeper insecurities, and that her difficulty with trust goes much further back in her life than her relationship with John. Only by addressing her own trust issues can she then engage in more meaningful ways to overcome and resolve her present jealousies. She would have to cultivate the character trait of *sippuk*, i.e., satisfaction with what one has and who one wants to become. Interestingly, I received a call from John two weeks after our lengthy phone call, requesting an appointment for himself and desire to resume therapy. I think it is safe to assume that he came to recognize that only he could deal with his reticence to express his feelings more openly and directly, and that his wife would have to find a venue to help her overcome her paralyzing jealousy, perhaps by eventually once again joining her husband in therapy.

A strikingly similar case involves another elderly couple, Thelma and Ralph, who I recently saw when they presented with a crisis in their marriage. Thelma began the session by saying that their daughter, Ariana, was married three weeks earlier and at the reception Ralph did not pay any attention to Thelma at all. She was distressed that he actually danced with their daughter's friend at a time when that particular dance was dedicated to dancing with "the one you love the most." Thus, it was clearly intended to be a dance for the bride and groom, and for others who wished to dance with their spouse. A short time later, she saw her husband once again dancing with that same friend of their daughter, and on another occasion, he was sitting at a table talking with her. She was extremely distressed by this, and since that time a high level of tension has persisted in the relationship.

Thelma went on to say that she and Ralph have been married thirty-one years, and they are always together in everything they do. This is the second marriage for both of them. Thelma is afraid that her husband's behavior may suggest that he would really rather be with someone else than her. She believes she may be especially sensitive to this because her first husband was unfaithful. At this point in time she finds it very difficult to be affectionate with her husband or even to spend time with him because of how deeply hurt she is by his behavior at their daughter's wedding. They have had an excellent marriage until these recent events, but at this point Thelma is so hurt and angry that she is fearful she may not be able to get beyond these feelings, thereby jeopardizing the future of their marriage. They came to therapy in the hope that they could work through and resolve this extremely intense conflict, which has left her feeling depressed and anxious, and him feeling hurt and angry.

Therapy appeared to have been going well during the initial sessions. They did their therapeutic homework reliably, such as writing role-reversal therapeutic letters which helped them see the issues from the other person's perspective. They were spending more quality time together talking and actively reminding themselves and the other how blessed their relationship has been for thirty-one years, and that one could see the situation from different points of view. Ralph acknowledged that he got carried away with his desire to show their daughter how happy he was for her, even admitting that, although normally a quiet, somewhat socially shy person, on this occasion—his daughter's wedding—he was feeling particularly good about himself and enjoying his role as father of the bride. He felt that he was the "man of the hour." He did acknowledge that his behavior was very insensitive to his wife, that he was thinking more of showing his daughter and everyone else how happy he was, but in the process neglected to include his wife or to even consider that he was "leaving her in the dust" in his efforts to show everyone his own joy. His need to "show off" embarrassed her, as they both have always valued living a life of modesty, avoiding any "flamboyant" or ostentatious behaviors. Even more distressing to her was his disloyalty—virtually abandoning her in order to "show off" and dance and talk with a "pretty young girl." This left her feeling unimportant to him. While it certainly appeared that progress was being made in terms of both of them being able to empathize with the other person's feelings, as soon as I began to even touch on the possibility that her feelings of jealousy may not be the only way to react to the situation, and that her reaction might be a bit excessive, she became defensive and angry—including at me—for in any way "challenging" her perception of the situation and her "right" to feel jealous. I tried to help her see that feeling "jealous," which is a feeling that involves seeing oneself as less important or less worthy than someone else, is a feeling which continuously fuels her pain. It is rooted in feeling that the other person has someone or something that you want but don't have. Instead, I tried to help her see that feeling hurt and angry at his disloyalty were more appropriate feelings, and that therapy could help her work through these feelings. But Thelma felt scorned, and it soon became a "badge of honor" which she "proudly" proclaimed anytime the issue came up. Not surprisingly, soon after the session in which I suggested her jealousy was mostly hurting herself, I received a message from Ralph saying that he and his wife would work things out and that they did not need to schedule any additional further sessions.

Sadly, jealousy was Thelma's "weapon" that she used to express her hurt and anger at her husband's disloyalty and lack of modesty at their daughter's wedding. She was not interested in "giving up" her jealousy yet, even though she knew that there was no actual "relationship" between her husband and their daughter's friend. His inability to fully "own" that his behavior was not innocent, as he tried to convince her it was, continued to fuel her jealousy. At this point in time, this unhealthy dynamic had more of a grip on them than their ability or willingness to look more closely at their own respective roles in perpetuating this toxic dynamic. The only way to continue to avoid looking inwardly was to stop therapy.

Kaas (Anger) versus *Yishuv Ha'daas* (Being Settled)

Rabbi Wecker

Anger is an especially despicable *middah*. *Sefer Orach Mesharim* notes that nothing positive is accomplished through fits of anger;[245] on the contrary, much harm is caused through angry outbursts.[246]

Rashbam observes that one easily angered is always on edge, and therefore can never truly appreciate and relish life.[247] This is sinful, for Hashem expects us to experience *simchah* and feel a sense of *hakaras ha'tov* (gratitude) to Him for his many *chassadim*, including, first and foremost, the gift of life itself.

Sefer Orchos Tzaddikim observes that anger causes even a wise person to act foolishly.[248] He is simply not in control of his intellectual resources during his fit of anger.

Rambam writes that human greatness is defined by one's cognitive ability.[249] Consequently, he adds that inebriation is a horrible sin, for it "ruins one's body and soul."[250] By extension, an angry person engages in similar self-destructive physical and spiritual behavior, and thereby undermines the very purpose of his existence.

---

245   See Talmud, *Kiddushin* 41a.
246   Authored by Rav Menachem Tarvish, published in 1858.
247   *Pesachim* 113b.
248   Gate 12, Anger.
249   *Moreh Nevuchim* 1:34.
250   Ibid., 3:8.

Sefer Orchos Tzaddikim continues sharing the litany of vices associated with anger. An angry person is unable to muster *kavanah* (concentration and contemplation) in his davening. *Kavanah* requires a settled and contemplative mood, which is impossible for an angry person to achieve.

Anger leads to arrogance, and an angry person will not admit to the truth if it contradicts his delusional self-perception.

An angry person is disliked by others and is a burden to his family and friends. People avoid attempting to influence him in a constructive manner since they do not want to deal with his emotional flare-ups. The result is that he lacks positive role models and influences.

The inability to interact positively with other people appears to be both a regrettable consequence of his angry disposition and a severe punishment for it. The Talmud lists a *metzora* (one afflicted with *tzaraas*, a disease that shares some similarities with leprosy, but is clearly a distinct, spiritual ailment) as "one of four categories of people who are considered (morally, not legally) dead."[251] Rav Chaim Shmuelevitz explains that the *metzora* is considered life-deprived due to the halachic requirement that he remain isolated from other people. His inability to relate to other human beings, to share in their joys, to commiserate with them in their sorrows, to bestow *chessed* upon others results in his being labeled as morally deceased.

One given to temper tantrums has, sadly, also effectively erected an emotional barricade between himself and the rest of the world. Regardless of whether or not it is due to a conscious act on his part, he suffers for his self-imposed sequestration from other people.

Rambam writes that due to its destructive nature, anger stands as an exception to a standard rule of *middos*.[252] As mentioned above, with regard to other *middos* (with the additional exception of *gaavah*), the golden mean is operative, i.e., one should aim to utilize these *middos* in moderation. For example, one should be neither a spendthrift nor a miser, but should instead strive to act with restraint between these two

---

251 *Nedarim* 64b.
252 *Hilchos Deos*, chap. 1–2.

extremes. Anger, on the other hand, is such a negative *middah* that one should endeavor to eliminate it entirely from one's personality.

The disposition to act in anger is not easily subdued. *Sefer Erech Apayim* quotes the great *gadol* Rav Yonasan Eibeshitz[253] as admitting that "on occasion I have stumbled and gotten angry."[254] The author notes further that an angry person finds it almost impossible to repent for his sins.[255] Anger leads to many serious sins, and effectively closes the door to *teshuvah* for those sins.

There are rare circumstances in which anger may be a justifiable emotion to express. A parent may sometimes feel a need to exhibit wrath to his child, and a *rebbi* may feel it essential to deliver a stern message to his student. According to the *Rambam* (above), one may only show a sense of anger, but ideally, may never actually experience the emotion of anger inwardly. *Sefer Orchos Tzaddikim* (see introduction), on the other hand, suggests that one may on rare occasions utilize the *middah* of anger.

SUMMARY

Anger is a dreadful middah, and easily leads to many serious sins. The angry person loses his ability to think rationally, to interact constructively with other people, to daven meaningfully to Hashem, and finds it incredibly difficult to repent.

With regard to anger, Rambam suspends the model of following the "golden mean" between middos; anger must be eliminated from one's personality.

Even great people at times succumb to feeling anger.

There are rare times where it may become necessary to express anger. Even then, many poskim claim that one may only exhibit a sense of fury, but he should never internalize the damaging emotion of rage.

Dr. Weissman

It's impossible to overstate the frequency with which *kaas*, the character trait of anger, surfaces in the therapy office. The reader should

---

253 He lived from 1690 to 1764.
254 Page 2, line 3 in the notes at the bottom.
255 Ibid., p. 48.

note that we are referring to the character trait of anger, as opposed to expressions of anger which might surface at moments of tension, but which are not characteristic of the person's typical reactions. We are referring to angry people, not a person who happens to feel angry. We have already seen a number of manifestations of *kaas* in our previous clinical vignettes.

Perhaps the clearest example of the destructive role anger plays was seen in our discussion of Roy and Courtney. During the first treatment episode when I met with them together, Roy's anger dominated the entire dynamic of the relationship, not only in terms of angry outbursts, but more insidiously, in terms of his arrogant demeanor—with frequent critical comments about his wife, kids, and almost everyone else peppering most of his communications. His capacity for empathy was overshadowed by his need to be "right" and to have things go the way he felt they should go, which translates into everyone having to do what he wants them to do. The damage done to his marriage and other relationships was serious enough for Courtney to insist on treatment, a position which required significant courage and strength. Enough progress was made in that initial marital therapy for them to resolve the crisis that brought them to therapy—their inability to reach an agreement about their wills. After weeks of verbally "sparring" with each other, arguing their "cases" for what they wanted the will to achieve, Roy dramatically (and unilaterally) delivered a proposal to give her what she wanted. He relished the credit for being willing to give her what she wanted, but it soon became apparent that all he really did was to make a concession. He had not taken any real steps to work on his chronically angry demeanor. He hadn't yet recognized the work on himself he needed to do.

But, after only a few months, Courtney *did* come to the realization of the work on herself *she* needed to do. To summarize from the presentation of her case earlier in this book, the work with Courtney early in individual therapy showed how therapy helped her develop tools to better handle her husband's angry outbursts and his controlling behaviors. In her present treatment, she is going a step further. She now recognizes that it is his *personality traits* which are at the root of the angry and controlling behaviors and she needs to learn how to deal with this. And, in order to be able to do this, she recognizes the need to work on some of her own character traits—persistence, strength, self-confidence, and self-worth. In fact, she has done some extraordinary work in her therapy. After a few sessions she began to express her feelings at the time he was engaging in some of the most troublesome behaviors, rather than suppressing her feelings and avoiding the conflict, while building resentment. She gradually helped him see the impact of his anger and controlling behaviors on her and the children, especially their son, and to help him develop a desire to become the kind of person who is able to restrain and process his anger before expressing it. He wanted to become a more loving husband and father. In one session, she reported how, while quietly talking one night, he apologized for all the mean things he has said and for all the hurt he knows he has caused her and the children. He then asked for forgiveness. She went on to say that Roy has come a long way in his efforts to be kinder and more thoughtful. It appeared to her that he was sincere, and she believes that he is trying to become a better person. The rest of that session focused on the importance of her finding the right balance between reinforcing these positive changes , while also giving him honest feedback when he says or does something hurtful. I expressed positive affirmation of how much she has persevered to be able to bring about this change in her husband.

There is another case I saw a number of years ago which captures the destructive potential of anger in the most graphic way. Jack and Meredith, a married couple in their early thirties with two young sons, came to therapy to deal with chronic tension and arguments in their day-to-day relationship. Much of the tension involved Jack's struggle to contain his anger when frustrated, both at home and at work. Although a dedicated father who also openly boasted of his love for his wife, his anger would often surface at the most inappropriate times, and in some instances, in a manner which was truly frightening to others. He gave much of his time helping to coach Little League where his two sons played on his team, but when a referee would make what he thought was a "bad call," he would get into a screaming match with the referee and on two occasions was actually kicked out of the game on a "technical foul" because of his outbursts. While he recognized his difficulty with anger, he felt that his wife's clingy dependence on her parents and her tendency to be too "soft" on the kids were sources of frustration to him. Many of their arguments stemmed from these specific issues.

On one particular occasion Jack and Meredith arrived for a marital therapy session obviously showing a high level of tension between them. Meredith began by saying:

> *I don't think I have ever been as upset at Jack as I was last night. You see, for a few days we had been having an argument over an old garden bench I wanted to give to my parents because I felt it was still usable. Jack felt it was not usable, so every time I would bring it to the backyard in order to take over to their house in our truck, he would pull it to the front yard for bulk pickup. This actually happened two or three times, with the bench going back and forth, until yesterday afternoon when he got home, when he saw the bench once again in the backyard. He was so furious that he took an ax and chopped the bench to pieces right in front of me and the kids, with them screaming in fear especially because I was also screaming at the sight of him being so out of control. When he finished, he threw the ax down and walked away pouting. Of course, after a while, things passed and at dinner things seemed kind of normal. He went in to check on the kids when they were asleep as he always does, and came out and apologized to me for losing his temper. He said that seeing the kids sleeping peacefully helped him feel not so badly about what they had witnessed several hours earlier.*

At this point in the session, I chose to intervene in a most direct fashion. I leaned toward him in my chair and in a quiet voice asked him if he knew what the boys were dreaming about while he was watching them sleep. He indicated that he did not know, but I told him that in all likelihood they were dreaming about him chopping up not only the bench, but maybe even mom and the two of them for screaming so much. I explained that in the unconscious mind, especially with children, that's how dreams work—something that bothers or upsets us during the day can surface in a dream in exaggerated form. The moment I pointed out the possibility that his sons were having the kind of nightmares I described, he burst into tears, sobbing while expressing his guilt and remorse over continuously doing this to his family and children. For the first time, he said how much he hates himself when he is this way, and that he's afraid his wife will kick him out and he will lose everything. This only makes him more insecure and intensifies his need to control, thus fueling the cycle. In this session, however, he seemed to "get it." He spontaneously expressed not only the recognition that he must change, but also the strong desire to change and to become a more patient, sensitive person who doesn't let his "arousal meter" instantly shoot up even with minor frustrations; he wanted to become a person who is able to respond calmly and thoughtfully even to stressful situations. This was a turning point in therapy, and we saw his efforts to shape and mold his character traits into those of the kind of person he would like to be increasingly effective and successful. Little by little, he began to transform into a more thoughtful, patient person who engages others.

In the foregoing discussion of four central negative character traits, which we saw manifesting in real-life therapy situations, one consistent underlying method I use to approach these situations is to create what I have come to call the "Yuck Response." This is certainly not a technical term. Rather, it refers to a moment when a person looks at something about his own character structure and says "Yuck! How could I be this way? How can I do such a thing? How could I be so selfish? How can I hurt someone's feelings without even thinking about it? How can I be so mean?" This kind of negative response to oneself, in which one comes to reject an aspect of himself that he/she now see more clearly, is a necessary step in the process of change. The actual clinical terms are taking something that is "ego-syntonic," meaning something the person is so accustomed to that they don't even notice it as part of their personality, and transforming it into something that is "ego-dystonic," such that the person has a visceral negative response to seeing that aspect of their own personality. It often takes a considerable amount of preliminary therapeutic work to get to the point where an individual is capable of seeing himself from this more objective perspective, but when it occurs, it can have the effect of freeing the person to now make choices about the kind of personality traits he/she truly wants to develop and cultivate. The parallel to this is when someone commits a sin and quickly comes to acknowledge the stain this places on their soul and the consequences in terms of G-d's "system" of reward and punishment for doing mitzvos (good deeds) as opposed to committing *aveiros* (sins). Indeed, the process of perfecting one's *middos*, i.e., working on one's character development, is part and parcel of the process of *teshuvah*—the way in which we repent for our sins, asking forgiveness from others whom we may have harmed, as well as forgiveness from G-d for violating or disrespecting His "rules for living."

There is an interesting paradox which seems to surface during the course of any individual psychotherapy. Often, an individual first comes to therapy with a complaint about something in their life which is causing them distress, with the goal of learning how to change whatever it is in their life (often another person such as a spouse or child) so they will no longer feel distress. The first challenge is to help the person see that the real work in therapy is not to "fix" somebody else, but rather to "fix" themselves. As we have seen, this process itself is complicated because at times the proper focus is on helping a person eliminate an undesirable thought, feeling, or behavior, but then the focus shifts to improving oneself by striving to internalize positive character traits, positive *middos*. In such a case, one is living a life of continuous personal growth. This leads to a much greater appreciation for the fact that each of us is responsible for our decisions, actions, and reactions, with increased awareness of his or her impact upon others.

Certainly, the transformation of a person from someone who blames outside circumstances and other people for their distress into a person who looks to himself to see how he can improve his reactions and decisions, and who strives for maximum personal growth and character development, is a beautiful process to witness. As a therapist, being a catalyst for this unfolding process is a remarkable privilege and is enormously rewarding. But, the journey shouldn't stop there. Becoming a person who feels a sense of internal peace and a desire for personal growth means always working to become kinder, humbler, and content.

As we saw at the beginning of this book, the Jews are considered "the Chosen People," but this is best understood to mean "chosen for a job"—to bring godliness into the world, and to live one's life strictly according to Hashem's "rules for living," i.e., strictly according to Torah. This is the way to be a role model who can influence others to also embrace such a life. Little by little, we "fix the world" first by fixing ourselves, and then applying our ever-evolving good character traits to influence the world. This is *tikkun ha'olam*.

TIKKUN HA'OLAM—PERFECTING THE WORLD

Dr. Weissman

Not surprisingly, we see a version of this spiritually-based perspective in modern-day psychological research and theory. A striking example of this is seen in the work of a renowned psychologist and researcher, Martin Seligman, who originated a theory that views depression as an emotional state which can result from "learned helplessness." From this perspective, when someone comes to believe that they are helpless to change anything in their life for the better, this sense of powerlessness undermines self-esteem, motivation, and in the extreme, even the desire to live. The "antidote" is "learned mastery." To the extent that one feels he has an impact on others, indeed, on the world, the more empowered he feels, resulting in improved self-esteem and a sense of fulfillment. Let's see what the Torah says about this.

Rabbi Wecker

In *Shemos* it states: "And Moshe said to the Jewish People: 'See, Hashem has singled out by name Betzalel, son of Uri son of Chur, of the tribe of Yehudah.'"[256] Rav Moshe Feinstein asked: What exactly are the people to take note of in the selection of Betzalel as the chief architect of the *Mishkan* (Tabernacle)? What possible message could his appointment

---

256   35:30.

have for the rest of the nation? Earlier in *Shemos*, we are informed of the consecration of Aharon and his descendants as *Kohanim*.[257] Yet, we do not find the term, *re'u* (see) utilized in that context.

Rav Moshe's answer is that one who is gifted by Hashem with a special talent is duty-bound to use that talent to serve both Hashem and His people. Even if no specific mitzvah pertains to that talent, there is a moral imperative to develop that talent to the fullest and use it constructively. Hashem blesses each of us with talents and abilities and bids us to utilize them for the benefit of others. This was the message of Bezalel's appointment to his new position. He utilized his talents to serve Hashem and humanity, and his example was meant as a model for us.

Rav Yosef Dov Soloveitchik offered the following insights into the obligation of *tikkun ha'olam*:

> *The modern Jew is entangled in the activities of the Gentile society in numerous ways—economically, politically, culturally, and, on some levels, socially. We share in the universal experience. The problems of humanity—war and peace, political stability or anarchy, morality or permissiveness, famine, epidemics, and pollution transcend the boundaries of ethnic groups. A stricken environment, both physical and ideological, can wreak havoc upon all groups.*
>
> *The responsibility of subduing the forces of nature and converting them into life-supportive energies was directed to Adam, the progenitor of all mankind. On the pasuk "Rule over the fish of the sea…and subdue it,"[258] Ramban adds: "He gave them (mankind) the power and the dominion over the earth to do as they wish with the cattle, the reptiles, and all that crawl in the dust, and to build and to pluck up that which was planted, and from the hills, to dig copper and other similar things." This mitzvah was addressed to all the descendants of Adam, Jew*

---

257 Chap. 29.
258 *Bereishis* 1:26–28.

and non-Jew alike. All are mandated to harness the forces of nature for the betterment of mankind. Jewish concerns are not exclusively parochial. It is our duty as human beings to contribute our energies and creativity to alleviate the pressing needs and anguish of mankind and to contribute to its welfare.[259]

A similar message is taught in the *Midrash Tanchuma*:

"When you come into the land and plant."[260] *Hashem said to the Jewish People: "Even though you find the land full of all bounty, do not say: 'Let us settle down and not plant.' Rather, be careful in planting, as stated: "And plant any tree for food."*[261] *Just as you came in (were born) and found plantings which others had planted, so you will plant for your children. Lest someone say: 'Since I am old and tomorrow I will die, why should I toil for others?'" Shlomo HaMelech said, "He has made everything beautiful in its time. He also has put eternity into their heart."*[262] *Eternity (ha'olam) is written defectively (without the letter vav). Why so? If Hashem had not hidden (read without the vav the word could be read he'elam, hidden) the day of death from people, a person would neither build nor plant. He would have said: Why should I persist in toiling for the sake of others? Hashem therefore shut off human hearts from death, so that one would build and plant. If he is worthy, it will be for him; if unworthy, it will be for others.*

A story is told that the emperor Hadrian was going to war with his troops to fight against a certain rebellious country. He found a certain old man who was planting fig saplings. Hadrian said to him: "You are an old man. Why are you persevering in taking the trouble to toil for others?" He responded: "My Lord Hadrian, here I am planting. If I am worthy, I will

---

259 Besdin, Abraham R., *Reflections of the Rav* (KTAV Publishing house, 1993), vol. 2, p. 75.
260 *Vayikra* 19:23.
261 Ibid.
262 *Koheles* 3:11.

eat of the fruit of my saplings; but if not, my children will eat." The emperor spent three years subduing the rebellion, and afterward he returned. What did that old man do? He took a fruit basket, filled it with the first-fruits of beautiful figs, and drew near to Hadrian. He said to him: "My Lord Emperor, take these figs, for I am the same old man whom you found when you were on your way to the war, when you said, 'You are an old man. Why are you taking the trouble to toil for others? See, Hashem has already found me worthy to eat some fruit of my saplings. Now this fruit in my basket is from those saplings." Hadrian said to his servants: "Take it from him and fill it with gold coins." And so they did. The old man took the fruit basket full of gold and began to go about his house boasting to his wife and children. So he told them the story…Therefore one should not cease from planting. Rather, just as he found this earth lush with vegetation, so one should still continue to plant, even though he is old. G-d said to Israel, "Learn from Me." He spoke by example, as it were.[263] "And G-d planted a garden in Eden, in the east."[264]

Rav Henoch Leibowitz noted from this Midrash that to preserve and enhance society is not only a *chessed* for succeeding generations, but also contains a degree of *chessed* to previous generations. Our forebears bequeathed to us a beautiful world, and we are duty-bound to prepare the same for those that will take over after us.

Another approach is that of Rav Simcha Wasserman. He notes the comment of the *Rambam*: "If not for the foolish people, the world would lay in ruin."[265] Rav Simcha explains that this world is developed by people who do not concern themselves with their certain death, but are instead intoxicated with the "dream of everlasting life." On the one hand, these people suffer from a tragic misplaced sense of priorities.

---

263 *Bereishis* 2:8.
264 *Vayikra, Parashas Kedoshim* 8.
265 In the *Rambam*'s introduction to his commentary on the Mishnah.

On the other hand, these people are the driving force behind the continuing settlement and development of the planet, something which benefits all of us.

Needless to say, this concept generates an additional responsibility that we have as Jews. We must ensure that the precious and sacred traditions of our Torah, that were transmitted to us in pristine state through the herculean efforts and martyrdom of our ancestors throughout the ages, is safeguarded through our indefatigable efforts for the next generations, until the hopefully imminent arrival of Mashiach, Amen.

SUMMARY

There is a Divine imperative for us to develop and hone our talents and skills for the betterment of others and society as a whole. To quote Rav Yosef Dov Soloveitchik: "It is our duty as human beings to contribute our energies and creativity to alleviate the pressing needs and anguish of mankind and to contribute to its welfare."

Just as our ancestors bestowed upon us a beautiful functioning world, so must we—out of gratitude to them, and out of a sense of responsibility to our descendants—continue this process of development and progress. An important corollary of this concept is that we must study the Torah and keep the mitzvos, and pass on this precious legacy to future generations.

Dr. Weissman

Randy is a thirty-five-year-old Caucasian male who came to therapy with multiple issues to address, including previously diagnosed post-traumatic stress disorder (PTSD) as well as traumatic brain injury due to multiple concussions sustained during his military career. He struggles with depression and anger management issues, and has a number of physical complaints, including chronic back pain and frequent migraine headaches, with these issues also stemming from incidents which occurred during his military career. He is presently considered to be 100% disabled and he received a medical discharge from the military due to these injuries and psychiatric problems. He came to therapy with the hope of dealing with these issues and the impact they have on his life. More specifically, he sought therapy, as he stated:

> ...to help me get control over my emotions, rather than feeling that I am always being controlled by my feelings and impulses. I've tried therapy before, even some marital therapy, but it didn't help. I'm seeing a psychiatrist at the Naval Hospital for medications, and I am going to anger management classes, but I really need someone to talk to, someone to help me figure out how to not react so badly to everything. I really want to become a better person.

Randy shared some important additional information, saying that he works for the Navy Wounded Warriors Program, explaining that he was medically discharged from the Marines, and presently the state of Virginia considers him 100% disabled, while the Department of Defense has concluded he is 80% disabled due to multiple physical and psychological problems.

> I also have chronic back pain and migraine headaches, and I had several concussions while on missions in Iraq and Afghanistan. I've been told I have TBI (Traumatic Brain Injury) due to being assigned to a fortified Navy transport vehicle which was going over rough terrain, and I was thrown all around in the vehicle. This actually happened twice. These deployments were really hard, always a lot of pressure. I saw a bunch of my friends killed. I remember a time when an officer blamed the death of one sailor on a good friend of mine, who in fact had done nothing wrong. I became really angry when I saw that officer falsely accuse my friend, and they actually had to restrain me so I wouldn't physically attack the officer. I still feel angry when I think about this, especially at this officer who blamed everyone but himself. I still have times when I go into a rage, and I have occasional blackouts.

He reported that when still in the Marines he received a negative evaluation, and he said that that experience totally changed him in a negative direction. He stated that he cannot turn his anger off since that incident, even with the help of medications. He said, "I can't stand being told that I did something wrong." I learned that he had the rank of sergeant in the Marine Corps, and that he also has a degree in homeland security. He complained that he still cannot get a job because of his physical problems.

At this point I inquired about family-of-origin issues, and he quickly revealed that he had an extremely traumatic childhood.

> *I was physically abused when I was a kid by my father, particularly when he was drunk, and he abused my sister also, but even when all of this abuse came to light no one did anything. We lived in poverty, and sometimes were sent to foster homes. My mother was a severe schizophrenic, who essentially left the family when I was five years old, possibly for a hospitalization, or maybe she just left us. I know she died from a brain tumor. My father abandoned the family when I was eleven years old, I think because he was drunk all the time. I lived alone at the house for two weeks with my sisters. Then we moved about to several foster homes. Then I moved in with my grandfather, and I lived there until I was seventeen years old and joined the Marines. My relationship with my grandpa was really close—he was always very warm and loving. He died two years ago. I don't think I've really gotten over that.*
>
> *Doc, the stress is killing me—I can't leave home without anxiety medication. My social life does not exist, and my wife cries a lot. She is also in therapy for depression. We really love each other and are very supportive of each other, but she just can't handle it when I get angry, and then we end up fighting and saying really bad stuff to each other.*

The therapy process with Randy has been (and continues to be) very challenging, with numerous "ups and downs," including verbal altercations at work, arguments with his wife, and two separate occasions when he stormed out of the office in anger when he felt I was "taking his wife's side" as we discussed recent arguments. Each time he left in anger, he would call or send me a text message apologizing and making sure I was still willing to work with him. Much of our work consisted of helping him acquire specific anger management tools, and over time his wife would join us for alternate sessions to help us address marital tensions. His motivation to change remained high, especially because his wife became pregnant during the course of his therapy. Also, he repeatedly stated how he doesn't want to be like his father, and that he wanted to be a really good dad. As a result of this high level of motivation, he *always* did his therapeutic homework and was able to take more and more control over his reactions to stressors and frustration.

Recently, a rather startling insight emerged in his therapy. Almost without exception, *everything* that triggered his angry reactions involved a situation in which Randy felt someone was doing something wrong—immoral, unfair, unjust, taking advantage, being selfish, etc. Usually, he would try to actively intervene in some way, often with disastrous results due to his overly harsh and judgmental posture. To his credit, over time he became increasingly receptive to my interventions, which often involved confronting him about the fact that his method of approach usually backfired when he was overly angry, harsh, and judgmental, and he would make matters worse instead of better. He was able to refine not only his method of reacting and intervening (when appropriate), but also his judgmental posture. He worked on giving others the benefit of the doubt, and came to understand that any attempt to intervene to correct a perceived "wrong" required doing so in a manner which conveyed love and caring for the person he was trying to correct. And, he was getting results! He was recently told he is being considered for an accelerated promotion at work, and his wife describes a more loving, caring husband who has less need to control or criticize her, and more of an automatic, "How can I help?" response to daily challenges and frustrations. Over time, Randy has evolved from a volatile, angry, argumentative person to one who is more thoughtful in his responses and reactions, pausing to consider the best course of action instead of responding reflexively to stressors. Although still "a work in progress," Randy stands out as a person who is now better able to channel his drive to "fix the world" into more controlled, measured, realistic, and effective opportunities to apply his own personal growth—his constant effort to improve his *middos*—into a life path of concern and caring about others and about the world around him, always trying to be a positive influence. He serves as a worthy example of an individual whose effort devoted to *tikkun ha'middos* progressed to an active focus on *tikkun ha'olam*.

EVED HASHEM—TO BE A SERVANT TO G-D

Rabbi Wecker

The epithet, *eved Hashem* (literally, "servant of Hashem"), is a label of honor bestowed only infrequently. Moshe Rabbeinu was accorded this title,[266] but as *Rabbeinu Bachya* notes, it was bestowed upon him only at the very end of his life.[267] During his life, Moshe was referred to as "a man of G-d."[268] *Eved Hashem* is a greater title, *Rabbeinu Bachya* concludes, since it implies that Moshe had continual access to Hashem, and was able to communicate with Him at will.

Rav Chaim Shmuelevitz discusses the concept of *eved Hashem* in three different *divrei Torah*.[269] He illustrates the deeper meaning of the concept by quoting a narrative from the Talmud.[270] The righteous Chizkiyahu, king of Yehudah, became deathly ill. The *navi* Yeshayahu came to him and said: "Thus says Hashem: 'Command your household, since you will die and not live.'"[271] What is the reason, the Talmud questions, for the redundancy of "you will die and not live"? The answer offered is that Chizkiyahu was informed that he would die a premature death in this world, and in addition he would forfeit his portion in *Olam Haba*. Chizkiyahu then inquired as to the reason for the severity of his punishment. Yeshayahu answered that the punishment was for his failure to bear children. Chizkiyahu responded

---

266 *Devarim* 34:5.
267 Commentary, ibid.
268 *Devarim* 34:1.
269 See *Sichos Mussar, Parashas Ki Sisa*, 4 Tammuz, and *Parashas Bo*.
270 *Berachos* 10a.
271 *Melachim* II 20:1.

that he saw prophetically that his children would be wicked, and he had therefore refrained from fulfilling the mitzvah of begetting progeny. Yeshayahu rejoined: "Of what concern to you are Hashem's secrets? Do as you are commanded, and Hashem will do as He desires."

Rav Shmuelevitz explains that Chizkiyahu's punishment was not merely for failing to fulfill the positive mitzvah of fathering children. Instead, the punishment was for Chizkiyahu's underlying attitude. One may not rationalize and reinterpret Hashem's mitzvos with the aim of not performing them; doing so results in a breakdown in one's relationship with Hashem. He is our Master and we are His servants, and a servant is expected to follow his master's command without attempting to second-guess its purpose. This is the hallmark of a true *eved Hashem*.

Along a similar line, Rav Shmuelevitz offers a new approach in understanding the test Hashem put to Avraham with His command to sacrifice Yitzchak (i.e., the *Akeidah*). The trial was not one of testing whether Avraham's love for the son of his old age, Yitzchak, was greater than Avraham's love of Hashem. Jewish history is replete with many examples of Jewish parents putting aside their deep-seated love of their children in order to fulfill the mitzvah of offering their offspring's lives *al kiddush Hashem*.

Instead, Rav Shmuelevitz notes that Avraham devoted his life to teaching people to love Hashem. He preached that Hashem is merciful and abhors child sacrifice. Avraham could have easily rationalized that the *Akeidah* would result in a *chillul Hashem*, and therefore he must not go through with it. Instead, he acted as a servant of Hashem, casting aside any rationalizations and doing exactly what Hashem commanded him to do.

A true *eved Hashem* is focused on only one task: fulfilling unquestioningly Hashem's will. Any thought of reward, even in *Olam Haba*, is simply not a consideration. The *Gra* is quoted as saying: "Even if the consequences were reversed, and the 'reward' for fulfilling mitzvos was Gehinnom (hell), and the 'punishment' for sin was Gan Eden (heaven), it would still be better to fulfill mitzvos."[272] The resulting reward or

---

272 See *Hagaon* by Rav Dov Eliach, vol. 1, pp. 231–232.

punishment is inconsequential to an *eved Hashem*; his focus is solely on fulfilling his beloved Master's bidding.

The Brisker Rav adds yet another layer to our understanding of *eved Hashem*.[273] He says: "One who has never sinned, but has looked for ways to exempt himself from being required to fulfill a certain mitzvah, is still considered a *tzaddik*. By contrast, an *eved Hashem* looks only for opportunities to fulfill mitzvos."[274] A true servant of Hashem looks for additional occasions to serve his exalted Master, and never attempts to discover any exemptions from his subjugation to Him.

Although these lofty heights of spirituality are not attainable for all but perhaps a few select individuals in our day, there is much that we can (and must!) accomplish. Our "to-do" list must include Torah study. It is only through studying Torah that we can gain an understanding of our obligations to Hashem. As one important example, the *Mishnah Berurah*, in the introduction to the laws of Shabbos,[275] quotes Rav Yonasan Eibeshitz as noting: "It is impossible to avoid *chillul Shabbos* (the desecration of Shabbos) unless one is well-versed in the laws of Shabbos, and has reviewed them a few times."[276]

Not only with regard to the laws of Shabbos, but in all areas of halachah (Jewish law) and *hashkafah* (Jewish outlook on life), we must look to our sacred Torah for true enlightenment and guidance.

Part and parcel of our Torah obligation is our duty to refine our character traits, and to act with sensitivity and consideration to all people. *Mesillas Yesharim* is considered one of the most authoritative works on *mussar*. Authored by Rav Moshe Chaim Luzzatto, the *sefer* opens with a unique introduction. This work, the author states, is not written primarily to teach anything new, but is instead meant to remind us of what we already know and understand fully. However, he continues, precisely because these truths are self-evident, people tend not to focus on them, and as a result, they are forgotten.

---

273 Rav Yitzchak Zev Soloveitchik, Rosh Yeshiva of Brisk Yerushalayim. He lived from 1886 to 1959.
274 *Otzros Rabboseinu MiBrisk*, p. 190.
275 Written by the Chafetz Chaim.
276 *Ya'aros Devash, Mishnas Dovid* edition, vol. 2, p. 85.

(It is possible that the author's words reflected, at least in part, great humility. The *Gra*, soon after purchasing *Sefer Mesillas Yesharim*, was quoted as saying that "a new light appeared on the face of the world, and that were the author still alive, he [the *Gra*] would travel by foot a great distance to greet him and get to know him."[277] Clearly, the great *Gra* found much that was original in this important work.)

It is critical for us to study and review with regularity the Torah teachings about perfecting our *middos*. *Sefer Chayei Adam*[278] states in the laws of Yom Kippur: "It is well understood that it is an absolute obligation to study *sefarim* that discuss *yiras Hashem* (the fear and service of Hashem) every day, whether a little or a lot."[279]

It is only through an ongoing and concerted effort that we can hope to refine our character traits and reach the great potential Hashem has given each and every one of us.

———— SUMMARY ————

An eved Hashem does not rationalize and reinterpret Hashem's mitzvos. A servant is expected to follow his master's command without attempting to second-guess its purpose.

Although these lofty heights of spirituality are not attainable for all but perhaps a few select individuals in our day, there is much that we can (and must!) accomplish. Our "to-do" list must include Torah study. It is only through studying Torah that we can gain an understanding of our obligations to Hashem.

It is likewise critical for us to study and review with regularity the Torah teachings about perfecting our middos. It is only through an ongoing and concerted effort that we can hope to refine our characters and reach the great potential that Hashem has provided each and every one of us.

Dr. Weissman

Rabbi Wecker's beautiful *d'var Torah* on *eved Hashem* pulls together a wide range of Torah sources to encapsulate the centrality of integrating

---

277 *Sefer Yarim Moshe*, pp. 46–47.
278 A halachic work authored by Rav Avraham Danzig. He lived from 1748 to 1820.
279 *Klal* 143, toward the end.

ongoing Torah study with the lifelong process of personal character development, *tikkun ha'middos,* and with the mitzvah of *tikkun ha'olam,* fixing the world. As I mentioned in the introduction to this book, I have come to realize that my approach to therapy has always been rooted in the application of Torah principles to the problems of daily living. The "guiding principle" in my work has always been to help each person I am privileged to work with to *embrace* the reality of *personal responsibility* for their actions, decisions, and reactions. I like to help my patients see that taking responsibility for how one deals with life, particularly how one deals with others, is not an onerous, burdensome undertaking, but rather a glorious ownership of G-d's greatest gift to us—freedom of choice! Responsibility. "Respons-ability"—is the "ability to respond." It is that freedom to choose which allows us to devote ourselves to perfecting our *middos* and to *tikkun ha'olam.* However, we must recognize that our purpose here is to fulfill G-d's will. We must see ourselves as obligated to make choices based on the eternal truths contained in G-d's handbook for daily living, the Torah. And, the truths are, indeed, eternal and universal.

IN CLOSING

Derech Eretz

Dr. Weissman

I ONCE HEARD SOMEONE TELL OF an occasion when the Rosh Yeshiva of a very prominent yeshiva was interviewing two highly praised candidates for entry into the yeshiva, together with two of his rabbinic colleagues. There was, however, only one opening available. They interviewed the first candidate, and he lived up to every accolade he received in his letters of recommendation. As soon as he left the room, the second candidate entered for his interview, and he also lived up to every accolade he received in his letters of recommendation.

A few minutes after the second candidate left, the Rosh Yeshiva announced that he had decided to admit the second candidate. In a most respectful manner, his two rabbinic colleagues inquired as to why the Rosh Yeshiva felt so strongly about the two candidates that he didn't even consider it necessary to ask either of them for their input. The Rosh Yeshiva answered: "I watched both candidates leave the building and walk to the parking lot across the lawn. The first one walked by trash on the lawn near a trash can without stopping. The second candidate stopped to pick up a piece of trash and put it in the trash can right beside him. He has the *middos* we want for this sacred yeshiva."

In his classic work, *Mesillas Yesharim*, Rav Moshe Chaim Luzzatto emphasizes a critical point which is sometimes overlooked, or perhaps not sufficiently emphasized. Namely, that what we refer to as *derech eretz*, meaning proper conduct, or good *middos*, is a prerequisite to "acquiring" Torah. In his introduction to his brilliant treatise on *Mesillas Yesharim* called *Lights Along the Way*, Rabbi Abraham J. Twerski, MD, cites numerous references that clearly emphasize this cornerstone of Jewish thinking. Rabbi Twerski cites a Midrash which states that "Torah and mitzvos were given for no other reason than to refine people's character."[280] Rabbi Twerski goes on to quote from the Talmud: "Had the Torah not been given, man would have been expected to learn proper behavior from observation of nature. He would have learned respect for private property from ants, modesty from cats, and fidelity from pigeons."[281] In response to the concern that man would have also acquired negative character traits from some animals, such as "rapaciousness from tigers, promiscuity from dogs, and vanity from peacocks," Rabbi Twerski cites a statement from *Koheles* in which Shlomo HaMelech states that "G-d created man with a sense of propriety, and that man would have been expected to exercise his innate sense of judgment to emulate desirable characteristics."[282] He then cites a verse which reads: "'G-d made man *yashar* (straight, simple, just),' and that very word, '*yashar*,' is contained in the title of the *Ramchal*'s monumental work, *Mesillas Yesharim*."

In the following *d'var Torah*, Rabbi Wecker pulls together a variety of sources supporting the primacy of *derech eretz* as the foundation upon which learning Torah—and *living* Torah—are based.

Rabbi Wecker

Noach expended herculean efforts on behalf of the animals that were his charges during the *Mabul* (the Great Flood). The Midrash notes that during the twelve months they lived in the *teivah* (the ark), Noach and

---

280 *Vayikra Rabbah* 13:3.
281 *Eruvin* 100b.
282 7:29.

his sons did not sleep at night.[283] They were preoccupied day and night with caring for the welfare of the surviving animals. Yet, the Midrash records that Noach and family did not exit the *teivah* at the first opportunity, when dry land appeared. Instead, Noach said, "Just as I did not enter the *teivah* without express permission from Hashem, so I will not exit the *teivah* without explicit authorization from Hashem."[284]

Rav Chaim Shmuelevitz explains that Noach acted with *derech eretz*.[285] *Abarbanel* explains that *derech eretz* is a Torah-mandated code of behavior that demands that we comport ourselves with etiquette (appropriate to that culture), ethics, and wisdom.[286] Once Noach entered the *teivah* with the sanction of the King (Hashem), *derech eretz* demanded that he await the King's consent before exiting.

The Midrash describes the severity of a failure to follow the moral imperative of *derech eretz*.[287]

> Any Torah scholar who does not possess understanding,[288] an animal carcass is more fitting than he. The proof to this idea is learned from the example of Moshe. He was the wisest of men, the greatest navi, the one who brought the Jewish People out of Egypt, the agent for many miracles wrought by Hashem in Egypt and at Yam Suf (Sea of Reeds), the one who ascended to the heavenly heights, the one who brought the Torah down from heaven, and the one who oversaw the construction of the Mishkan (the Tabernacle). Yet (even though he possessed all of these qualities), he did not enter the inner sanctum of the Mishkan until Hashem summoned him, as it states: "And Hashem called to Moshe."[289]

Rav Shmuelevitz noted that *Parashas Pekudei*, which details the inauguration of the *Mishkan*, states nineteen times that the *Mishkan* was

---

283 *Parashas Noach* 9.
284 *Bereishis Rabbah* 34:4.
285 *Sichos Mussar, maamar* 4.
286 Commentary on *Avos* 2:2.
287 *Vayikra Rabbah* 1:15.
288 *Radal* commentary clarifies this as *derech eretz* and humility.
289 *Vayikra* 1:1.

constructed "as Hashem had commanded Moshe." Moshe's primary role in the creation of the *Mishkan* was obvious. Yet, despite Moshe's intimate involvement in practically every facet of its construction, Moshe would not enter the *Mishkan* until Hashem beckoned him to come. The dictates of *derech eretz* cautioned him to await Hashem's directive before entering.

Rav Shmuelevitz also notes that the Midrash equates understanding with *derech eretz*. They are intimately intertwined: one either possesses both, or he inevitably possesses neither.

The imagery of the "animal carcass" is meant to teach us, according to Rav Moshe Sternbuch,[290] that just as the stench of decaying meat serves to warn people to keep away, so too do the actions of a *talmid chacham* who acts without understanding serve to turn people away from interacting with him.

Rav Aharon Kotler clarifies that *derech eretz* is itself an integral part of Torah.[291] Without mastery of that section of Torah, however, it is impossible to gain proficiency in any other part of Torah.

Derech eretz also encompasses a sense of self-respect. Rav Reuvain Grozovsky quotes the comment of the Talmud that one who eats a meal in the marketplace acts in a way that is comparable to a dog.[292] Some rabbis say that he is also ineligible to serve as a witness. *Rashi* comments that since he is unconcerned with his own honor, he may well be dishonest.[293] Rav Grozovsky explains that even though this person has not committed even one sin, he has lost his presumption of being an upstanding person. He may appropriately be suspected of dishonesty. Since he shows no concern for himself, there is no guarantee of his integrity.[294]

Rav Yosef Dov Soloveitchik discusses the halachah that one may not pass by a synagogue during *tefillah* times.[295] The rationale is that one who observes his behavior may suspect him of deliberately avoiding

---

290 Vice president of the Eidah HaChareidis in Yerushalayim, b. 1922.
291 Rabbis B. Wein and W. Goldstein, *The Legacy* (Jerusalem: Maggid, 2013), p. 38.
292 *Kiddushin* 40b.
293 Ibid.
294 See *Sefer Maamarei Rebbi Reuvain, maamar* 43.
295 Based on *Berachos* 8b.

participation in *tefillah b'tzibbur* (communal prayer). Rav Soloveitchik explains that the underlying principle here is that "the reputation of a person does not belong to him...If he will fall in his reputation...a human personality is desecrated...(H)is spiritual personality doesn't belong to him, (and) neither does his reputation."[296] The Torah exhorts us: "And you will be clean of sin before Hashem and Jewry."[297] Our reputation, just like our very lives, belongs to Hashem.

The Slabodka Yeshiva laid great emphasis on what was called *gadlus ha'adam*, the greatness of a person. Humans were created in Hashem's image. Our innate greatness does not allow us to simply rest on our laurels, however. Along with the great privilege we were granted by Hashem comes an unending responsibility to live a lifestyle that accords with His wishes. Along those lines, Rav Henoch Leibowitz once observed that the only thing that keeps us from sinning and debasing ourselves is our sense of human dignity.

Rav Grozovsky concludes that development of one's *middos* and *derech eretz* is the principle purpose of the creation of humanity. In another *shiur*, he adds that negative *middos* are the prime cause of a person's failure to follow the Torah's dictates.[298] *Middos* and *derech eretz* are of such supreme importance, he says, that many Rishonim wrote many *sefarim* on the subject, each one of which offers a unique perspective on the strong link between mitzvah observance and *middos* and *derech eretz* refinement.

Rav Soloveitchik is quoted as having said: "There can be no Judaism without morality."[299] He quotes the Midrash: "Rabbi Reuven was asked the following question by a philosopher in Teveria:[300] 'Who is the most despicable person in the world?' Rabbi Reuven answered, 'An atheist, since the denial of all social norms follows in its wake. No man sins unless he first rejects Hashem.'"[301] Without the moral imperative of

---

296 Holzer, David, *The Rav: Thinking Aloud* (Holzer Seforim), *Sefer Bamidbar*, pp. 236-237.
297 *Bamidbar* 32:22.
298 *Maamar* 65.
299 *Reflections of the Rav*, vol. 1, p. 195.
300 Tiberias, Israel.
301 *Tosefta Shvi'is* 3:5.

the Torah directives, one can rationalize and relativize any and every act. Perhaps it might be appropriate to add then that there can be no morality without the Torah.

SUMMARY

Derech eretz is a Torah-mandated code of behavior that demands that we comport ourselves with etiquette (appropriate to that culture), ethics, and wisdom. The actions of a talmid chacham who acts without understanding serve to turn people away from interacting with him. Derech eretz is itself an integral part of Torah. Without mastery of that section of Torah, though, it is impossible to gain proficiency in any other part of Torah.

Derech eretz also encompasses a sense of self-respect. One who eats a meal in the marketplace acts in a way that is comparable to a dog. Some rabbis say that one who does so is ineligible to serve as a witness. Rashi comments that since he is unconcerned with his own honor, he may well be dishonest as a witness. Even though he has not committed even one sin, since he shows no concern for himself, he loses his presumption of being an upstanding person. There is no guarantee of his integrity.

Our reputation, just like our very lives, belongs to Hashem.

The only thing that keeps us from sinning and debasing ourselves is our sense of human dignity. The development of one's middos and derech eretz is the principle purpose of the creation of humanity.

Without Torah directives, one can rationalize and relativize every act. Perhaps it might be appropriate to add then that there can be no morality without the Torah.

Dr. Weissman

We have come full circle, back to the premise of this book which, as mentioned in the introduction, is conveyed by its title:

> *Therapy According to G-d conveys the underlying theme of this work, namely, to show how Torah emerges constantly in the clinical setting of the psychotherapist's office, which itself is a microcosm of life's struggles shared to some degree by all of us, offering the very basis of any and every therapeutic intervention.*

Of course, there is no intent to imply that the insights contained in this book are limited to the kinds of problems which present in the psychotherapy office. On the contrary, we are really addressing human behavior in general, including how we conduct our relationships, and society itself is dependent on the values and lessons contained in the Torah. From the therapist's perspective, every issue brought to the therapy office is addressed through the prism of Torah, regardless of whether the patient is Jewish or not, because the "handbook for living" contains all of the principles underlying psychological theories and the application of those principles to guide the therapist in his or her effort to help the patients resolve internal distress and to improve the quality of their relationships with others.

It is a tree of life to those who hold fast to it.[302]

---

302   *Mishlei* 3:18.

About the Authors

RABBI MORDECHAI WECKER studied for many years under the guidance of Rav Henoch Leibowitz, *zt"l*, at Yeshivas Rabbeinu Yisrael Meir HaCohen (Chofetz Chaim Yeshiva) in New York and Israel, and thereafter under the guidance of Rav Moshe Feinstein, *zt"l*, at Mesivta Tiferes Yerushalayim in New York. He was awarded *semichah Yoreh Yoreh Yadin Yadin* from Rav Feinstein. Rabbi Wecker also received a Master of Education with a concentration in school administration from Cambridge College.

Rabbi Wecker has been a *mechanech* (Jewish educator) for over forty years. In addition to teaching both school-aged students and adults, he has served as head of school at Jewish day schools in Massachusetts, Pennsylvania, and Virginia. Rabbi Wecker has given *shiurim* on the weekly *parashah* and the siddur throughout his career. In 2000, he was awarded the prestigious Pillar of Maimonides award from the Maimonides School in Brookline, Massachusetts. He presently resides in Baltimore, Maryland.

Rabbi Wecker takes special delight in the warm personal relationships he develops with his *talmidim*, saying that "I am most proud of the fact that many of my students keep in touch with me long after their graduation."

He may be contacted at mowecker@outlook.org

MICHAEL S. WEISSMAN, PhD, received his undergraduate education at Princeton University, graduating magna cum laude in 1970. He went on to earn his Master of Science (1972) and doctorate (1974) degrees from the University of Massachusetts in the field of clinical psychology. He completed a postdoctoral fellowship at Upstate Medical Center in Syracuse, New York before moving to Virginia in 1975 to take a position as the first doctoral-level psychologist at the local Community Mental Health Center. Following that, he was employed by a private psychiatric inpatient and outpatient facility, where he founded a psychology internship training program, which qualified for full approval by the American Psychological Association after only three years, and served as director of this program. He also held the position of Director of Psychological Testing. In 1981 Dr. Weissman chose to leave that large clinical facility in order to open a "solo" private practice. Although never anticipating expanding beyond a solo private practice, within a year another therapist asked to be able to see patients in his practice. He was followed by many others over the years, asking to be a part of this growing practice, often citing a reputation for quality care as well as extremely high ethical standards. Currently, the practice has a total of eighteen therapists and three office locations. Throughout his professional life, Dr. Weissman has always been involved in local and state psychological associations, and has held the positions of president of the Tidewater Academy of Clinical Psychologists and president of the Virginia Academy of Clinical Psychologists.

As a *baal teshuvah*, Dr. Weissman has embraced the challenge of integrating a Torah lifestyle into his every activity. It did not take long to "see the Torah" in his work as a psychotherapist. He is continuously inspired by the recognition that "every intervention I offer to my patients directly stems from some aspect of Torah which applies exactly to what that particular patient needs at that particular moment." He feels immeasurable gratitude to Hashem for leading him to a profession in which every hour of every day is an opportunity to share Torah in ways that directly improve the quality of life and relationships for the many patients he is privileged to serve.

Dr. Weissman can be contacted as msweissman@cox.net.

About Mosaica Press

MOSAICA PRESS is an independent publisher of Jewish books. Our authors include some of the most profound, interesting, and entertaining thinkers and writers in the Jewish community today. Our books are available around the world. Please visit us at www.mosaicapress.com or contact us at info@mosaicapress.com. We will be glad to hear from you.

In honor of

RABBI WECKER AND DR. WEISSMAN

two respected and inspiring friends

SENDER AND CHAMIE HABER
NORFOLK, VA

Dedicated to the memories of

ABRAHAM AND SYLVIA WINTMAN

pillars of the Jewish community in
Malden and Brookline, Massachusetts

BY THEIR CHILDREN

COMPLIMENTS OF THE ITZHAK FAMILY